FAME (fām) *n.* 1. The condition of being known to many people. 2. A good reputation.
—famous *adj.*

Also by Michael Flocker

The Metrosexual Guide to Style
The Hedonism Handbook

The
FAME GAME
HOW TO MAKE THE MOST OF YOUR 15 MINUTES

 *Michael Flocker*

Da Capo Press
A Member of the Perseus Books Group

Illustrations by Scott Magoon
Text design by George Restrepo
Set in 10-point Bulmer

Library of Congress Cataloging-in-Publication Data
Flocker, Michael, 1963–
The fame game : how to make the most of your
15 minutes / Michael Flocker. —First Da Capo Press
ed. p. cm.
ISBN-10: 0-306-81424-2 (pbk. : alk. paper)
ISBN-13: 978-0-306-81424-2 (pbk. : alk. paper)
1. Fame—Humor. 2. Celebrities—Vocational guidance—Humor. I. Title.
PN6231.F29F66 2005
818'.607—dc22 2005010047

First Da Capo Press edition 2005

Published by Da Capo Press
A Member of the Perseus Books Group
www.dacapopress.com

Da Capo Press books are available at special discounts for bulk purchases in the U.S. by corporations, institutions, and other organizations. For more information, please contact the Special Markets Department:

Special Markets Department
Perseus Books Group
11 Cambridge Center
Cambridge, MA 02142
(800) 255-1514
special.markets@perseusbooks.com

Contents

Of course, popular culture is such that one always has a choice regarding the degree to which one buys into the hype. Do you need to be a star to get ahead in life? No. Do you need to dazzle on a daily basis to have any hope of one day having a healthy bank account? No. But it's not a bad idea to study what's going on here. There's no denying that the Western world is entirely obsessed with celebrity, so just as the handyman conceals miraculous implements in his private tool box, you, too, should have a few little weapons at your disposal to drag out in times of necessity or emergency.

If you become an accidental celebrity, take a loan and strap yourself in. You'll need a media handler who can help craft sound bites, a grief counselor who also books TV shows, an agent, a contract lawyer, a ghostwriter, an accountant, security guards, Capitol Hill contacts (should there be a need for the passage of a relevant law), a suitable wardrobe, and a good haircut (for public appearances).
   —**Maureen Orth,** ***The Importance of Being Famous***

By understanding the modern science of celebrity you can also give yourself a nice little edge in the job interview, a seductive advantage in the realm of romance, or the simple confidence to pull focus in your direction at will when the occasion warrants. What used to be considered indefinable magic is entirely ripe for deconstruction, and once you build up the tricks in your arsenal, the grand game of life takes on a whole new twist as you selectively and responsibly manipulate your way to the top.

Ooh, listen. Can you hear the distant voices muttering that such notions are shallow and superficial? Well, of course they are. Any sane person recognizes that, but you and I both know that most people rarely see below the surface. In your personal relationships, love affairs, and friendships, you'd better be seeing beneath the surface or you're totally screwed, but in the competitive landscape we call "society," there have always been superficial laws and rules.

Is there not country-club etiquette? Does corporate culture not have a spirit-squashing code of conduct? Aren't television appearances all about sound bites? Yes, yes, and yes. These things are a given, and life today is really no different than it was in Victorian times when propriety and denial were the assumed points of view. By understanding one's times and the dynamic of the day, one has the power to realize one's dreams, be they small or obscenely large. Throughout history, those who have succeeded have played the game and given the public what they wanted. The clever ones always did it with tongue firmly planted in cheek, but they understood that charm is the key to the kingdom, much as a password might have gotten you into the speakeasy when things were gloomy.

I say all of this with complete awareness that there are those who will surely frown upon our little scheme to advance you and your agenda. But I must say, I'm very pleased that you have found this book, because you are different. You know there has always been something that sets you apart. Sure, there's a whole slew of dullards out there who will pick up this book, and don't get me wrong, I love the book sales, but you, in particular, are the one I was hoping to reach. There is something entirely unique about you that, frankly, you haven't taken advantage of. So, we'll look back in time and see what has worked for others, we'll plot a few strategies for the future, and wc'll draw upon your inner well of charisma, which has heretofore remained untapped. This is going to be so good for you.

Of course, the principles and advice contained in this manual are entirely universal and can benefit anyone who wishes to make a slightly larger splash during their time on the planet. Knowledge is power, history is revealing, and life is very, very good when you know what you are doing. So, let us all see how we can apply the principles of popular culture and celebrity to our own lives, selectively utilized in order to amp up our personal biographies.

The truth is that stars are everywhere. The most easily identified among them are the international film stars, the superstar athletes, and the charismatic politicians who rise above the rest of the pack. However, they may also be the coworker down the hall who is shooting up the corporate ladder, the New York artist who is bathed in "buzz," or the saucy newlywed who just moved into the trailer park and is inspiring a torrent of gossip and resentment among the other wives. But the attention they attract and the whispers they generate are not accidental.

In this modern age of supreme self-awareness and personal branding it would appear that a little investigation might be worthwhile. After all, there are currently six billion people roaming the globe and that is a lot of competition. So whether you want to rule the world or just ooze a little more charisma at the next office party, you'll need to stock up that tool box and learn the rules of the fame game.

At the end of the day, as in all things, it is quite unnecessary, and more than a bit embarrassing, to live your entire life aspiring to be a "star." But who wouldn't benefit from a little extra magnetism, a touch more charm, or the ability to turn heads without having to dance naked on a bar? Wouldn't you like to be able to turn on the charisma as easily as you flip on a light switch? I thought so. So, let's see how you can polish up that sad old bag of bones you call yourself.

(Not you, babe. You're fantastic. That was directed at the others.)

CHAPTER

WHO ARE YOU?

I pretended to be some-body I wanted to be until finally I became that person. Or he became me.

—CARY GRANT

Well, Hello There!

So, what about you? Are you a self-confident head-turner reading these words with a knowing smile and a raised eyebrow? Or are you more of a dreamy wall-flower, timidly turning these pages and hoping fever-ishly that the advice contained herein will not require you to unbutton anything? Most likely you fall some-where in between these two extremes, and really, that's the most sensible place from which to begin.

In any case, the first order of business here will be to evaluate your current level of luminosity. One must have a clear understanding of where one stands on the grand blaze-o-meter in order to determine whether baby steps or giant strides should be taken. Eventually, by the time you finish this book and fling it carelessly across the room, you should be ready to stride out the door ablaze with confidence. But first, let's answer a few questions with complete honesty, to see where we stand. And honesty counts. A serious undertaking such as this should not begin under fraudulent circumstances. We will learn about fraud and artifice later on.

Evaluating Your Star Potential

Take a moment to review the following list of twelve probing questions, and place a numerical score next to each of them, using the key below. Once you are satisfied that you have answered them all in good conscience, total your score and see what the results reveal.

NEVER: *1 point*
NOT OFTEN: *2 points*
SOMETIMES: *3 points*
USUALLY: *4 points*
ALWAYS: *5 points*

_ Do people tend to turn and notice when you enter a room?

_ Do you enjoy being photographed?

_ Are you aware of others who radiate charisma?

_ Are you confident when meeting strangers?

_ Are you aware of how people perceive you?

_ Are you confident enough not to care?

_ Are you good at flirting?

_ Do you approach strangers socially?

_ Do you know when you are being watched?

_ Do you dress to impress?

_ Are you a good listener?

_ Do you target people you want to meet?

Now, add up those points, and see where you stand:

12–20 POINTS: You are dangerously close to being invisible. Rush out and buy another copy of this book in case you misplace the first one.

21–30 POINTS: Your charisma is barely detectable to most. You are lacking in confidence, and you must pay very close attention.

31–40 POINTS: You may be seen, but you are not always noticed. You are teetering on the brink of being average, but you have sufficient awareness to rescue yourself.

41–50 POINTS: You've got a little something going on there, and are a work in progress with good potential. Enjoy the book and concentrate on the subtle stuff.

51–60 POINTS: You are either wildly sexy and devastating or completely deluded. Read on and you will find out which of these is true.

So, how did you do? Was your score embarrassingly low? Don't worry. You're a blank canvas and things can only get better. Did you land somewhere in the middle? Good. There's room for improvement. Or did you score magnificently, you big fat star? If so, this breezy read should entertain and confirm everything you've always believed. That is, if you can keep that gigantic head of yours from causing you to tip over and roll off the couch.

It's never too late to be who you might have been.
–George Eliot

Taking Stock

If there is one thing that everyday stars are keenly aware of, it's what they have tucked away in their personal portfolio of charms. Like investment bankers, they identify their assets and leverage them for all that they're worth. So take a page out of their proverbial book … Got a dazzling smile? Then flash it when you're in trouble, but use it sparingly. Are you fantastic in bed? Then let that be the foundation for your confidence, but keep the source a secret. If your intellect is your greatest strength, then increase your power by observing and recognizing opportunities, or if your personal style is your greatest weapon, then work it as if you had no idea you looked so good.

Everybody has something to work with. It may be something of genuine worth, or it may be entirely superficial. Ideally, you will have several strong qualities to draw upon, but you can't do anything with them unless you identify them and take ownership of them. And bear in mind, all of these attributes can be cultivated, so that in time, your personal portfolio may be bulging obscenely. So, how many of these attributes do you have to begin with?

Wit	*Sensitivity*
Beauty	*Intuition*
Sex appeal	*Fashion sense*
Warmth	*Humor*
Charm	*Sexual confidence*
Mystery	*Intellect*
Shyness	*Charisma*
Boldness	*Determination*
Spontaneity	*Edge*
A great body	*Style*

WAITING FOR THE FAME BUS: *According to the Harris Interactive Poll #43, dated August 9, 2000, 30 percent of all adults think it likely they will be famous for fifteen minutes.*

Circle the qualities that are innate in you, and place a check mark next to those that you would like to cultivate in order to form a more complete package. These traits will help you determine the archetype that you will most likely embody as you come to define yourself and boost your level of popular appeal. Obviously, the more you have, the better off you are, but if you confuse the qualities you want with the qualities you truly have, you are prematurely sliding into self-delusion. Be honest.

Archetypes

In all forms of storytelling, in novels and plays and films, there are archetypes. There is the hero, the sidekick, the gatekeeper, the mentor, the trickster, the herald, and so on. Archetypes are the standard characters upon which all drama is based. And all stars are aware that life is a drama, and that they are characters in a larger scenario. But archetypes are not stereotypes. An archetype is no more than a very loose-fitting, malleable role that can be custom-tailored to suit your own desires. And knowing which archetype best suits you is a key element in defining who you are and what you represent.

It is important to point out that we are not speaking here of pigeon-holing ourselves. That would be counterproductive as individuality is perhaps the single most important quality one must cultivate in order to truly shine. To be unique is to have power. But to understand one's basic archetype is to identify one's course. One need only look to the stars to understand how archetypes work. And by speaking of "the stars" we are, of course, not speaking of something so dreary as the heavens. No. We are speaking of Hollywood!

Julia Roberts is the girl next door. Sure, we'll allow her an occasional dramatic role, but really only once in a while. We want her to be goofy and laugh that laugh. Nicole Kidman is the ice princess. Yeah, she can be funny, but we'd rather see her corseted up and frosty. Cameron Diaz is the perennial party girl. No period pieces for you, cutie, thank you very much. Tom Cruise is the ace—ace pilot, ace spy, ace lawyer, ace samurai, ace bartender even! Tom Hanks is the regular guy, and that's why America loves him. It's hard to believe he could ever be a villain. And Johnny Depp is the bohemian, a quirky, sensitive soul whom we hope never to see covered in sweat, dangling precariously from a cable as he rescues the world from God knows what. We have our perceptions of our stars, and these people are at the top of their field because they know how the public perceives them and they have found their niche.

In the arena of contemporary music you have the pop tart, the heart-throb, the good girl, the bad boy, the gloomy sensitive girl, the suave crooner, the rebel party guy, the monster-freak, and so on. But archetypes exist beyond Hollywood and the music industry. Think of high school. There were the jocks, the stoners, the freaks, and the band geeks. In the office there is the hot shot, the slacker, the uptight priss, and the ass kisser. Like it or not, in every social milieu people adopt roles or they simply fall into them by way of other people's perceptions.

Now, in the real world, people are not one-dimensional, but as far as everyday reactions go, you have already been pegged. The good news is that attention spans are shorter than ever, so reinvention is always an option. So, take a moment to review the classic archetypes below and see who you believe people perceive you to be. Not who you want to be, but who people think you are.

CIRCLE EACH ARCHETYPE THAT APPLIES:

A-Lister   *Athlete*

Achiever   *Big Shot*

Bohemian	*Jet-Setter*
Charmer	*Outsider*
Clown	*Party Animal*
Daredevil	*Player*
Diva	*Rebel*
Fashionista	*Rising Star*
Flirt	*Schmoozer*
Heartthrob	*Siren*
Hipster	*Socialite*
Hottie	*Sophisticate*
Hunk	*Stud*
Insider	*Subversive*
Intellectual	*Vixen*

Now go back and place a check next to the archetypes you'd *like* to embody. Do the checks and the circles match? If they do, then your course is clearly laid out. If not, a little renovation of the self may be in order.

What Is Talent, Anyway?

Regardless of the attributes you possess and the archetypes you embody, you will require some degree of talent in order to make use of them. Over the course of several decades, America's admiration of rarefied talent slowly but steadily morphed into an obsession with imagery. Today, the teenage twink with a strong management team is elevated to national celebrity, while the classically trained virtuoso musician sits unrecognized in the third row of an obscure orchestra, unable to afford dry cleaning. For many, this is yet another sign of the decay of Western civilization, and to those who appreciate the integrity of art and place a high premium on classical training, this is a disappointment indeed. In the minds of others, art is nothing more than a reflection of the society in which we live.

In any case, defining talent has always been tricky business. But if history has taught us anything, it is that talent and training are not the same thing, and this holds true in all arenas. You do not need to study music theory at a prestigious university to release a bestselling rap album, nor do you need a master's degree to become the CEO of an international corporation. However, you do need to know what you are doing, you need to know what you are good at, and you need to educate yourself in order to execute.

The important thing to remember is that instinct, intuition, and a strong sense of self can take you very far indeed. And maybe that's what talent is. But regardless of what your talents may be, sitting around waiting to be patted on the head for them will get you nowhere. And spending your life trying to get validation by having other people recognize your talents is also pointless. What you need are direction, purpose, and goals. They may be grand or humble, but they need to be clear.

The Power of Intention

Let's assume you're an actor. Do you want to become a film star? Is that really your goal, or do you simply love acting? Do you find true creative satisfaction on the stage or in being part of the filmmaking process? Would you still do it if you knew you'd never get rich? Or is the dream to become famous and wealthy so that your arrival on the red carpet is greeted with a blaze of flashing lights and screams of adoration? If it's the latter, you are already on some seriously shaky ground.

It is perfectly reasonable to want to do well in life and to achieve financial security. It is also reasonable to want to be admired by others. But if you choose acting, or any other field of endeavor, with only a distant dream of flashing lights and giddy euphoria, you are in for some serious disappointment. That is not a goal, it is a fantasy. You will never jump from the starting line to the top of the heap, and you will never be "discovered" and whisked off to fame and fortune. Success is achieved over time by taking incremental steps that build on one another. And those who cave the first time they encounter a roadblock are guaranteed to fail.

"Such tough love so early in the book?" you ask. Well, yes. This is not a course in miracles. We are speaking here about the qualities of successful people, and they are those who succeed despite the odds, not because they have been granted a free pass. The people who succeed in life, on any level, tend to have a clear understanding that they are embarking on a very long road. Through determination and willpower, they make choices that lead them in the right direction, but they are rarely delusional. At least not at the outset. Save your crazy bag for later.

The important thing to grasp, here and now, is that there will never be a point at which you break through some imaginary wall, are embraced by the masses, and all your problems fall away. All the money in the world cannot erase your self-doubts, there are no guarantees, fame is not love, and no one is immune to life's ups and downs. If you can truly accept that and still decide to forge ahead with optimism, excitement, and belief, then you are in very good shape.

Anything is possible in this life, and the choices and decisions you make on a daily basis will largely determine the outcome, but your motivation is all-important. If you are motivated by greed, need, or selfishness, it's probably not going to happen. If you are doing what you do because you love it, you have something to say, or you have a vision you want to realize, you might succeed beyond your wildest dreams. Then again, you might not, but you're far more likely to enjoy the ride regardless of the outcome. A writer writes, a painter paints, and a skier skis—wherever they can.

Open Windows

In every lifetime, there are windows of opportunity that open up, and it is those who recognize the importance of such opportunities and have the courage to jump through those windows that usually

I have an everyday religion that works for me. Love yourself first, and everything else falls into line.
–Lucille Ball

go on to the greatest of successes. Hesitate and that window may close forever. Of course, impulsive decisionmaking is to be avoided, but when you are faced with a dream opportunity that you know is right, it is a very sad thing when fear and indecisiveness cause the dream to slip away.

Often the fear that prevents us from leaping is a fear of change. When a chance at success presents itself, there are those who will jump at the very first opportunity. But there are also those who shrink back, afraid of the unknown and insecure about their ability to meet the challenge. For these people it would seem that the distant dream is merely a comforting fantasy, and the reality of achieving that dream is a threat to their safe little world of comfort and low expectation. Never let yourself fall into that latter category. There is absolutely no justification for fear of success.

So what if you've never done anything like it before? Here's your chance. Don't worry about failing or looking foolish. The only real failure is not trying. I mean, what's the worst that could happen? That last question is rhetorical, by the way. Don't start imagining horrible scenarios—put that energy toward preparation.

The point is that if you want to change your life, then you may have to change your ways. If a golden ring presents itself, you should reach for it. If you don't, you will be sitting in a sticky puddle of regret for a very long time. Just remember, it's always better to jump through a metaphorical window than out a real one.

DO be courageous and seize opportunities for advancement.

DON'T waste time volunteering for those crap jobs no one else wants to do.

DO make alliances with those who can help you.

DON'T ignore everyone else or your plan will be hopelessly transparent.

DO step out of your comfort zone from time to time.

DON'T obsess about failure. It's an essential ingredient in the recipe of success.

Planning Ahead for Immortality

As you plot and scheme your way to immortality, noble motivation securely in place, there is one question you need to ask yourself early on in the game. Just how colorful and richly textured will your autobiography be? If your life were to eventually become the subject of a movie or documentary, how would you be portrayed, and by whom? How will you encourage your grandchildren to lead their lives to the fullest if you have no story of your own to tell?

Regardless of your current star potential or preferred archetypes, it is important to understand that your story is already under way. That sad and lonely childhood, the doomed relationships, the ill-fated early marriage(s), those questionable decisions you made back when you were low on cash, these are all scenes in the larger movie that is your life. Of course the same holds true for your triumphs over adversity, your personal achievements, and all of your various journeys, adventures, and love affairs. With that in mind, it is important to remember that you are continuously in the process of creating your own legend (or in some cases, a precautionary tale).

Though it is the life you lead that will ultimately script the legend, it is your personal duty to maintain a scrupulously documented archive of your existence on the planet for those who may follow and seek to discover your true story. Not everyone is lucky enough to be appreciated in his or her own lifetime, and if this is true for you, when the time comes for your story to be told, you can still exert a creative hand from the grave controlling the imagery and highlights that are used to tell your story. Then again, if a documentary is made while you are still alive, you can generously offer up a wealth of flattering or insightful items with which to fill the screen.

THE KEY IS SIMPLY TO BE PREPARED. AND IN THIS CASE, BEING PREPARED MEANS KEEPING RECORDS AND EDITING SELECTIVELY:

Set aside and preserve the most flattering photographs of yourself from various stages of your life. If necessary, have them cropped to remove goofy relatives or tacky surroundings.

Save a single photograph for each major milestone in your life. Graduation, competitions, marriage, significant journeys, and profound friendships should all be preserved. They'll make you seem human.

Keep all significant letters and/or correspondence. While love letters can be very touching, rejection letters are even more significant. Any letter notifying you that you are hopelessly out of your element or that you should give up your dreams makes an amusing keepsake when you ultimately prevail.

Carefully preserve all significant wardrobe items. These might include wedding dresses, uniforms from your worst job ever, erotic costumes, horrendously dated outfits, and your most gaudy jewelry. They will provide context.

Journals are infinitely valuable, not only because they document your story, but also because they document the shifting ways in which you perceive your own story over time. Do not document any criminal activities.

Childhood items of note can add a touch of sentimentality to the collection. But don't get carried away. While a president's teddy bear may seem oddly poignant, a trunk full of stuffed animals and toys is just creepy. Be selective.

Be sure to include manuscripts of any kind. Even in an unfinished state, musical compositions, short stories, screenplays, and novels can all contribute to a valuable impression of unrealized genius. Then again, you may drag them out yourself and finish them someday.

Press clippings of any kind are worthy of preservation, with the exception of police logs noting that you drove over a mailbox. Of course, once stardom is attained, such things preserve themselves and only early mentions of your rise to stardom are of any interest.

Over time, the value and significance of your personal archive will become apparent. After all, you're going to need something with which to fill that hometown museum, right? And if the museum never happens, it's still a very nice gift to yourself to keep a collection of items that reflects your unique life story. Even if it's gathering dust in the attic, there will come a day when you want to look back and your personal treasure trove will ultimately tell a clear and colorful story that might otherwise have been lost.

So, now that we've had our little pep talk, you should know who you are, and who you want to become. But before you begin to plan the archives, let's see what we have to work with in terms of raw materials.

CHAPTER 2

A small hat size is 21 1/8 21.5 inches around

A medium hat size is 21 7/8–22.25 inches around

A large hat size is 22 5/8–23 inches around

An extra-large hat size is 23.5–23 7/8 inches around

An extra-extra-large hat size is 24.25–24 5/8 inches around

Really, it's quite simple. It's just Darwinism at work. Why do the off-spring of celebrity couples so often end up with careers in film or television? It's not so much a question of nepotism or even talent as it is a question of genetics. Two attractive big-heads get together, and that results in a baby big-head who is genetically predisposed to a career on camera. Athletes merge with athletes, and that produces physically gifted, unsuspecting infants whose future careers as athletes are speculated upon before they can even walk. Then there are the ugly rock stars who hook up with supermodels. Invariably those kids get the mother's height and the father's looks. Bum deal.

But the important thing to understand is that, in a wildly competitive world, your genetic lineage may hold the key to the professional path best suited to you. There are always pressures and expectations thrust upon the children of superachievers, but if you have the good fortune to be born to anonymous parents, you can evaluate your inherited traits and determine the professional path most suitable for you. So, how might you best cash in on your Darwinian inheritance?

HUGE HEAD; SMALL, TAUT BODY; SEXUAL AVAILABILITY:
Move toward the silver screen. You'll need a touch of talent to stand out among the myriad other big-heads, but you're sporting the physical formula for success.

TOOTHY SMILE, THICK HAIR, NONTHREATENING SEXUALITY:
Television is your preferred medium. Minimal acting ability and a likably goofy demeanor will help secure employment on a sitcom.

VERY TALL, VERY SKINNY, BIG LIPS:
Modeling is your milieu. Beauty is always enhanced by drama, so secure a progressive hairdo and let a fierce attitude conceal your shaky interior.

CONSIDERABLE HEIGHT, NO MUSTACHE, A MASSIVE EGO:
Politics is your bag. Height implies authority, a clean appearance suggests good morals, and the smile of a sociopath will serve you well.

MUSTACHE; BAD SKIN; A SMALL, BLACK RAISIN FOR A HEART:
You have the makings of a world-class tyrant. The mustache (on a man or woman) signifies evil, and a supremely bad attitude based on insecurity is your ticket to short-lived domination.

SHORT LEGS, THE ABILITY TO SPIN IN PLACE, FROSTED HAIR:
You are doomed to a life in the Ice Capades. Sorry.

EXTENSIVE PLASTIC SURGERY, HAIR EXTENSIONS, COLORED CONTACT LENSES:
This is the formula for a "career" as a dim-witted socialite. Of course, you'll need to sleep around, say dumb things, and spend much of your inheritance on your wardrobe.

NOTABLE BODY PARTS, UNUSUAL FLEXIBILITY, A COMPLETE LACK OF SHAME:

You're a porn star, pussycat! Education, moral compass, and long-term vision not required. Best to focus on securing a sugar daddy/mama because a hard rain is gonna fall.

THREATENING SEXUALITY, RHYTHM, A GREAT ASS:

These are the makings of a pop star. The ability to sing is less important than the ability to vamp, but the key is to write your own songs, if you can. The publishing royalties will keep you going long after your ass sags and the public gets tired of you.

GOOD TEETH, GOOD HAIR, NORMAL TORSO, ASS AS BIG AS YOU LIKE:

Stay in school and you could be a news anchor. Most news is still considered serious, so you will need a good vocabulary, but if you can avoid the long shots, you can eat until your thighs explode.

BAD HAIR, SIGNIFICANT HEIGHT, INTENSE STARE, AN EGO THE SIZE OF MONTANA:

You might one day become a CEO of a major corporation. Of course, sociopathic tendencies, ruthless ambition, and emotional detachment are also required. Try to remember the little people.

They used to photograph Shirley Temple through gauze. They should photograph me through linoleum.

–Tallulah Bankhead

Did you not find your physical formula on the list? No worries. These are only the traditional stereotypes. As we know, shrewd ambition and shameless self-promotion trump all when it comes to the old scratch-and-claw. In fact, if you can transcend conventional wisdom, as well as your physique, and make your mark as a trailblazing iconoclast, you will eclipse them all. And really, just between you and me, that's the way to go.

Personal Style

TINY TERRORS

Objects on the screen may be smaller than they appear:

Dolly Parton
5'

Carrie Fisher
5' 1"

Bette Midler
5' 1"

Reese Witherspoon
5' 2"

Prince
5' 2½"

Martin Scorsese
5' 4"

Al Pacino
5' 5"

Dustin Hoffman
5' 6"

Tom Cruise
5' 7"

Kurt Cobain
5' 7"

Jon Stewart
5' 7"

James Dean
5' 8"

Lest there be any squawking at this point about the unfairness of genetic limitations, we shall now examine an area in which each of us has complete control. Regardless of your natural endowments, the way that you present yourself and the image you project are infinitely more important that your inherited physicality. Just as you have now determined your archetypal tendencies, you must develop an understanding of how best to enhance and accentuate your new persona.

You know perfectly well that in today's world, appearance matters. Well, actually, it has always mattered. Masks and uniforms have been employed for countless centuries to convey and control the subconscious visual messages we send out. Military uniforms convey the strength and unity of an army. White wedding gowns convey purity and innocence. And the standard dark suit conveys reliability and professionalism in the workplace. Throughout history, public images have been carefully constructed by and for those who rise to positions of power or great influence.

Though few of us may attain global influence, the power of your own physical image should not be underestimated. Now that you have defined yourself as a hottie/diva/rebel or a charmer/outsider/rising star, you'll need to put a little lipstick on the pig, as they say in advertising. You're not the only hipster/daredevil/player out there, so you need to set yourself apart. Now, this doesn't mean that you need to go all flash and start wearing feathers to the office. Let's not self-destruct before we get started here. Your personal signature may be as subtle or as loud as you wish, and it should never be so strong that it makes you uncomfortable.

The process of developing your personal style involves no more than a quick evaluation, a choice of direction, and a little flourish of creativity. What are your best physical assets? What are your worst physical assets? How can you accentuate the positive and minimize the negative? Answering just a few key questions should help you define your direction:

EVALUATE:
WHICH OF THE FOLLOWING TRAITS DO YOU WANT TO CONVEY?

Power	*Mystery*
Sensuality	*Intelligence*
Humor	*Softness*
Edge	*Strength*
Sophistication	*Masculinity*
Flash	*Femininity*
Dignity	*Androgyny*

Circle any three and keep them in mind as your personal pillars of style.

AVERAGE ALTITUDE

According to a report from the Centers for Disease Control and Prevention, the average heights for U.S. adults in 2002 were:

*Male
5' 9 ½"
Female
5' 4"*

DIRECT:

DECIDE ON A DIRECTION FOR YOUR STYLE TRANSFORMATION. WHAT DO YOU NEED TO DO?

Tone down	*Slim down*
Add excitement	*Bulk up*
Loosen up	*Minor tweaks*
Tighten up	*Major renovation*
Add boldness	*Accessorize*
Soften the edges	*Minimize*
Update	

Circle any action items that may help you to begin your transformation.

CREATE:

WHAT TOOLS ARE AVAILABLE THAT YOU CAN USE TO ADD A PERSONAL STAMP TO THE PICTURE?

Hairstyle	*Patterns*
Hair color	*Textures*
Makeup	*Fabrics*
Eyewear	*Tailoring*
Colors	*Shoes*

Jewelry	*Strength training*
Outerwear	*Aerobics*
Underwear	*Diet modifications*
Exercise	*Vice elimination*
Weight loss	

Circle three or more, and use them as concrete ways to express your best inner self.

The circles that you have drawn should enable you to plot a course of action. The changes may be made over time or you can dive right in and get those renovations under way today. Once you know what you want to project, and you have identified what you need to do and how to do it, you are up and running. But there are other aspects of your physical self to consider.

Playing Up (or With) Your Ethnicity

Embrace your heritage, people! It's a large part of who you are and taking pride in your cultural background is not only psychologically healthy, it can also be very beneficial in the fame game. Dignity and pride are two qualities that are universally appealing, and any attempt to downplay one's social or ethnic background is not only pointless, it is socially irresponsible. Your race, creed, color, nationality, and cultural upbringing are all part of a much larger, complex tapestry that makes you completely unique in the world. And therein lies a great source of personal power.

I came out here with one suit and everybody said I looked like a bum. Twenty years later Marlon Brando came out with only a sweatshirt and the town drooled over him.
—Humphrey Bogart

And while it is important to embrace and appreciate one's heritage, one should never be confined by it. Stereotypes, racism, sexism, prejudice, and general bigotry are experienced on some level by nearly everyone, though admittedly to varying degrees. But in any situation, the way we react to them largely determines the degree to which they affect us. We can be intimidated, or we can move forward with dignity and confidence, transcending stereotypes and allowing those very qualities that make us supremely unique to slowly unravel the misguided preconceptions we encounter.

That which makes you different is that which makes you strong. And being underestimated can actually work to your advantage if you recognize the opportunity. Prove them wrong. Make them rethink their mind-set. Charm the shit out of them until they wish to God they could be more like you.

By understanding people's preconceptions, you can play with them, spin them, and deconstruct them. There is no need to pretend to be anyone other than who you are. Behold the basketball superstar from China, the white rapper from Detroit, the black supermodel with the British accent. There's really nothing terribly surprising about any one of them, except to those with preconceived ideas. And look at you. You've got a few nice contrasts going on, haven't you?

So, mix things up. We're all international mutts to some degree; don't limit yourself. You don't have to be Scottish to wear a kilt any more than you have to be Japanese to wear a kimono. You are who you are, but that doesn't mean you can't enjoy every aspect of any culture on earth. *(This does not apply, however, to the forty-five-year-old Jewish music executive who insists on dressing like a gangsta rapper. That's just wrong.)*

Excelling at Elocution

One of the essential ingredients of success in any field is the ability to communicate clearly and effectively. If you can't communicate clearly, you can't be understood, and if you can't be understood, you will rarely get what you want in life. But effective communication goes beyond a big vocabulary. Your vocal tone, your speech patterns, and your regional accent all play a part in the overall package.

A distinct accent, whether regional or foreign, can work both for and against you. At best, a nice accent can be endearing, exotic, and even sexually provocative. At its worst, an awkward accent can be a huge liability that keeps you from being taken seriously. The desirability of various accents is largely a subjective matter, but a smooth southern drawl is very different from a hillbilly twang. And foreign accents can range from the sensuous to the absurd depending on whether they are controlled or sliding into parody.

In acting schools and communications classes, the general benchmark by which "proper" speech is measured is known as Standard American English, which is a generalized American accent that is thought to be free of any identifiable regional inflections or pronunciations associated with particular dialects. Basically, it's the accent most national TV hosts employ. Most people prefer to retain a reasonable facsimile of their original speech patterns as a stamp of individuality, though some actors and public speakers may need to free themselves of their regional speech patterns in order to make themselves more marketable.

The key is to truly understand how you sound, and to make a conscious decision as to whether your particular (or perhaps peculiar) accent is an asset or a handicap. Is it charming or is it horrendous? If you're not sure, just read a newspaper article into a tape recorder and play it back. It should all become clear quite quickly. If a little modification is in order, there are plenty of books, tapes, classes, and speech therapists out there to help. But in trying to improve your speech, you must always be wary of drifting into affected speech patterns. Attempts to sound vaguely European or somehow "upper crust" tend to backfire more than they succeed. Chances are your affectations will be largely transparent and will thus lead to snickers and ridicule rather than admiration and enchantment.

The actual tone and quality of your voice can also make a big difference in how you are perceived. High-pitched voices are generally considered unappealing in both men and women. Nasal voices come across as whiny and negative. Speak too loudly and you'll send the message that you're overbearing. Speak too softly and people may think you are weak. Happily, most of us can make vocal adjustments in our speech with a little practice and commitment. By reading out loud at home you can experiment with a lower register, or work on your enunciation, and eventually bring that high-pitched squeal down to a nice velvety level.

Public Speaking

It is said that more people fear public speaking than fear death, and it's true that the mere idea of giving a presentation or a speech can bring a trickle of pee to the leg of the strongest among us. However, one of the defining qualities of successful stars is their ability to seize the spotlight and shine therein. If speaking in public comes easily to you, that's great. If it terrifies you, that's too bad. It's a fear you'll simply have to conquer if you want to seize control of your destiny. As with skydiving, you just have to jump out of that plane.

If necessary, you can always start small. Offer a toast at a wedding or ask a question at a public meeting. In time, you can graduate to making speeches or presentations. You don't want to wait until your first televised interview to experiment with such matters. You won't be amused when your friends are playing the videotape over and over again laughing their heads off.

IN ANY FORM OF PUBLIC SPEAKING, TRY TO KEEP THE FOLLOWING IN MIND:

No one's life is at stake. It's not nearly as important as you're making it out to be.

A very deep breath beforehand helps to slow the heart rate. And remember to keep breathing as things proceed.

Physical contact with your surroundings will help center you. Feel the wood of the podium. Check the strength of the armrests on the chair. This will bring you out of your head and into the physical space.

Make eye contact with your interviewer or your audience. The instinct to avoid eye contact only makes you feel more isolated and panicky. By making contact with individuals you will have something to hook into.

Don't rush. Speak slowly and deliberately, and take time to think. The pauses are not as long as you think they are, so don't fall into the trap of filling them needlessly with "um"s and "ah"s.

Beware of fidgeting and moving around. Find a comfortable position, whether standing or seated, and just let gravity do its thing.

Pee beforehand.

Style is knowing who you are, what you want to say, and not giving a damn.
—Gore Vidal.

Moronisms to Avoid at All Costs

If you are going to speak in front of people, or even when you are speaking to people, there are certain faux pas of grammar and pronunciation that can undermine your credibility faster than a drop of the pants. The heinous abuses of language listed below may seem painfully obvious to someone of your particular intellect and breeding, but they are woefully common. So, just for fun, scan the list to make certain you aren't committing any of these ghastly gaffes:

I COULD CARE LESS: No. The idea here is that you care so little, you "couldn't care less." If you say, "I could care less," then you are stating that you do care.

IRREGARDLESS: This is not a word. You are combining *regardless* and *irrelevant*. Please cease and desist. The word is *regardless*.

ALL THE SUDDEN: I know it seems crazy, but many people actually say that and it drives me up a wall. Things happen "all of the sudden."

WORLD WIND: This would be a global breeze. If things are swirling about you, that is a whirlwind.

LITERALLY: *Literally* means *actually*. If he "literally" bit your head off, you wouldn't be able to tell me about it.

FROM BAD TO WORST: No. There is a step in between. Things go from bad to worse.

ALL INTENSIVE PURPOSES: Unless you're describing your workout regimen at the gym, the phrase is "all intents and purposes."

ME VS. I: There is a time for *I* and a time for *me*. You send an e-mail to Bob and me. Bob and I will send one back. Just remove Bob from the sentence, and there's your answer.

ASTERIX: This is not the correct pronunciation. There is no x. The third syllable is pronounced like the word *risk*. Think of it as the danger of an incoming comet—aster-risk.

EXPRESSO: Again, there is no x. There never was one, and there never will be. Whether you order a single or double shot, and no matter how fast you'd like it served, thank you very much, it's still *espresso*.

YOOGE: The h is not silent in the word *huge*. The building is not YOOGE, it is huge. The same holds true for *humor* and *humid*.

NUKE-ULAR: Despite the high-level mangling of this word on a regular basis, it is pronounced "noo-klee-ar."

Now, having made such an issue of grammar, it seems only fair to throw in an old joke that illustrates the pomposity of being just a bit too linguistically uptight:

A young freshman from a small town is making his way across campus on his first day at an Ivy League school. Slightly disoriented, he stops a fellow student and asks, "Excuse me, but can you tell me where the registrar's office is at?" The upperclassman winces and says, "Well, I can tell you that at this university we don't end our sentences with prepositions." The younger student thinks for a moment and responds, "I'm sorry. Can you tell me where the registrar's office is at, asshole?"

Plastic Surgery

At this juncture, we come to the inevitable and humorous discussion of cosmetic enhancement. It's a dramatic shift of topic to be sure, but it is both sociologically and culturally worthy of review. Though mostly confined to Western culture, plastic surgery provides a fascinating window into the modern human psyche. When it comes to the business of show, it's a fairly safe bet that virtually every major celebrity in Hollywood has had something done, but plastic surgery is not limited to Tinseltown. In ever-escalating numbers, people around the globe are having their bits lifted, tightened, or sculpted, or having new bits inserted.

ACCORDING TO THE AMERICAN SOCIETY OF PLASTIC SURGEONS:

More than 8.7 million cosmetic-plastic-surgery-procedures were performed in 2003.

Botox injection was the overall top cosmetic plastic surgery procedure, with more than 2.8 million procedures performed in 2003.

The five most popular cosmetic surgical procedures were nose reshaping (356,554), liposuction (320,022), breast augmentation (254,140), eyelid surgery (246,633), and facelift (128,667).

In 2003, buttocks lifts increased 74 percent from 2002.

Forty-five percent of cosmetic-plastic-surgery patients were repeat patients in 2003.

Who Be Snippin'?

According to the International Society of Aesthetic Plastic Surgery, the following countries, listed in order of number of precedures, account for 68 percent of the world's plastic-surgery procedures:

USA

Mexico

Brazil

Canada

Argentina

Spain

France

Germany

Japan

South Africa

LOVE YOUR STYLISH LITTLE MAN-BAG!

The latest plastic-surgery trend sweeping through Hollywood is said to be the testicle lift. For Hollywood hunks getting a bit long in the tooth, a pert little teabag makes for a nifty confidence boost.

Ghouls Just Wanna Have Fun

With nifty little web sites like AwfulPlasticSurgery.com available for all the world to peruse and chuckle over, it is important for the modern-day star to remember that one's personal renovations can easily be tracked and publicized as light entertainment. Again, subtlety and self-restraint are of paramount importance should one decide to tighten things up a bit. The sad truth is that the public is generally unforgiving of saggy celebrities, so we expect a few nips and tucks from those in the public eye. However, when one's surgical procedures begin to eclipse one's accomplishments, one enters a whole new realm of clowndom. Now, as a serious cautionary exercise, let's review a select few whose dysmorphic disorders have caused them to dive-bomb into surgical superstardom:

MICHAEL JACKSON: Obviously in a league of his own, the former black man, now white woman, still maintains that there were only two nose jobs, and only to correct a sinus condition and a subsequent singing disorder. Well, of course. Why would anyone suggest otherwise? That's crazy. She looks perfectly natural.

JOCELYN WILDENSTEIN: Manhattan's infamous socialite, once unkindly dubbed "the bride of Wildenstein," gave an entirely new meaning to the quaint old phrase "cat lady." Determined to achieve the look of the feline beasts she so adored, she succeeded. But, alas, she has become internationally known for all the wrong reasons. Still, I'm sure she's a darling.

JOAN RIVERS: This brassy comedian turned red-carpet reptile and made a career of pointing out who looks awful. Ironic. Though she does have the good sense to acknowledge and poke fun at her own plastic proclivities, one can only hope she will always be able to afford a personal assistant to administer the eye drops as she sleeps corneas to the wind.

CHER: One must grant Ms. Sarkisian-Bono-Allman-now-single-forever-thank-you a little slack. Having maintained a career that has spanned five decades, she has always been utterly forthright concerning her personal upgrades. She who says in an interview, "If I wanna sew my tits on my back, it's nobody's business," can pretty much be forgiven anything.

DOLLY PARTON: Another celebrity who understands the power of self-deprecating humor, the bulbous Dolly has always said, "It takes a lot of money to look this cheap!" So, there you have it. No denials, no attempts to fool anyone. She's just giving us the cartoon we all want from her, and for that, we applaud her.

From these five brief examples, we can draw two lessons. The first is that self-awareness and unapologetic honesty go a very long way when it comes to endearing ourselves to the masses, regardless of the issue in question. The second is that becoming a cartoon can be very profitable, but only if you're in on the joke and are entirely comfortable with the persona you are presenting to the world. Otherwise, you become the joke.

But enough of this unseemly business. You will require no such surgical alterations. At least not yet. First, we must delve into that fascinating psyche of yours and see if there aren't a few adjustments to be made inside that big starlike head.

CHAPTER **3**

CONFIDENCE

You have to believe in yourself, that's the secret. Even when I was in the orphanage, when I was roaming the street trying to find enough to eat, even then I thought of myself as the greatest actor in the world.
—CHARLIE CHAPLIN

The Populebrity Index

Before we begin our sobering dissection of what confidence is really all about, it is worth pointing out that a loathsome person with all the confidence in the world is still going to be loathsome. Now likability, in and of itself, does not equal success, nor is it required in life to get ahead. But if you can manage to win people over and swing them to your side rather than bulldozing them, you will find that you'll get a lot more help along the way to the top. So let's begin by assessing your level of populebrity.

Populebrity is the direct correlation between how well you are known and how well you are liked. Ideally, your levels of celebrity and popularity will both be very high. For example, Mike Myers is recognized around the world for the goofy but lovable characters he portrays on-screen, and he is generally considered an extremely likable star. Thus he has a very high degree of populebrity. On the other hand, you take someone like, oh, I don't know … just off the top of my head … say, Paris Hilton. She has gained international fame, and though she is good for an occasional chuckle, she is not generally considered beloved. Hence, it could be said that Ms. Hilton suffers from a lower degree of populebrity.

Of course, not everyone is recognized around the globe. In fact, most people are not known far beyond their family, friends, neighbors, and coworkers. But the question is, what is your current level of populebrity in that little pond of yours? Are you aware of your own charisma? Do you know who you are? Do you know how others perceive you? Should you be more famous than you are, given your innate star quality? Or are you widely recognized, but unable to create a favorable impression among others? Let's try a little calculation and see where you currently stand.

BASED UPON THE DESCRIPTIONS BELOW, DETERMINE WHERE YOU FALL ON THE SCALE AND CIRCLE THE POINT VALUE IN EACH COLUMN. DON'T LIE AND DON'T BE MODEST:

DEGREE OF RECOGNIZABILITY	DEGREE OF LIKABILITY
10 *World famous*	*Universally beloved* 10
9 *You have fans*	*Loved by nearly all* 9
8 *Recognized by strangers*	*Extremely popular* 8
7 *Known in many circles*	*Well liked and respected* 7
6 *Reasonably popular*	*Liked by most* 6
5 *People remember me*	*Liked by some* 5
4 *Known only to family and friends*	*Tolerated by most* 4
	People don't understand me 3
3 *People tend not to remember me*	*Notoriously unlikable* 2
2 *Reclusive*	*Detested by all* 1
1 *Completely anonymous*	

ADD THE TWO FIGURES TOGETHER. THIS IS YOUR BASE VALUE. NOW, IF ANY OF THE FOLLOWING DESCRIPTIONS APPLY TO YOU, ADJUST YOUR SCORE AS INDICATED:

NEW IN TOWN: *Add 1 point*
RECENTLY BROKE UP: *Add 1 point*
PROMISCUOUS: *Add 1 point*
QUICK TEMPER: *Subtract 1 point*

BELLIGERENT DRUNK: *Subtract 1 point*

DRUG PROBLEM: *Subtract 1 point*

All you need in this life is ignorance and confidence, and then success is sure.

—Mark Twain

NOW YOU HAVE YOUR INDEX NUMBER. WHAT DOES IT MEAN?

0–4: HOPELESS.

> *You must get therapy immediately.*

5–9: CHIN UP.

> *You are either a likable agoraphobe or a famous asshole.*

10–14: NOT BAD.

> *A low score for a celebrity, but good for a star on the rise.*

15–19: VERY NICE.

> *There's something shameless about you, isn't there?*

20–23: STOP LYING TO YOURSELF.

Confidence and Intention

All right, having established your starting point, we can now examine the building blocks that may help you raise that score. If you are going to realize your true star potential, you'll need a lot more than dumb luck.

It should come as no surprise that, above all else, confidence is the single most important quality shared by successful people in any field. But how exactly does one acquire confidence? To many, it seems to be little more than an irritatingly elusive gift bestowed upon some and denied to others. But this is a false assumption. Confidence does not spring randomly from the ether, nor does it come from a deeply rooted belief that one is in possession of superior talents or universal appeal. That, my friends, is known as conceit.

So, why did Charlie Chaplin believe, even as a child, that he would be the greatest actor in the world? And what's up with these wildly successful people who always say that they knew they were somehow different, that they would do something spectacular one day? How could anyone know such a thing, you ask? Was it a psychic vision? Probably not. Encouraging parents? Well, that never hurts, but it's not enough.

Always bear in mind that your own resolution to succeed is more important than any other one thing.
—Abraham Lincoln

We all know that the need to achieve on a grand scale is often a reaction to deeply rooted childhood issues. Absent parents, narcissistic mothers, overbearing fathers, attention-grabbing younger siblings, cruel teachers, mean peers, or any number of other childhood influences can plant a wildly competitive seed early on and inform a lifelong compulsion. But compulsion is not the same thing as confidence.

Confidence comes from a combination of intention and determination. It is not so much a condition as it is a decision. Sure, confidence can come from knowing you are physically beautiful, sexually attractive, or devastatingly charming, but such forms of confidence can come easily undone when there is nothing beneath the surface. For confidence to bring about actual results, there must be an unshakable intention that is driving the actions.

Whether you are interviewing for a job, auditioning for a part, or merely attending a cocktail party, you need to have in your mind a realistic purpose. To approach any of the scenarios listed above thinking only, "I hope they like me," is not a foundation upon which confidence can be built. Your intention may be small or large, but it needs to be clear: "I am going to charm the interviewer"; "I am going to make the casting director laugh"; "I am going to flirt with that person I've had my eye on."

Of course, the larger objectives are also important. After all, you do want the job. But by focusing on your smaller intention, the pressure of getting that job, landing the role, or meeting the love of your life is reduced to a manageable level, and you are far more likely to make a good impression overall if you are not radiating life-or-death desperation because you've decided on an all-or-nothing outcome. If you don't get the role, at least you made them laugh, and they may call you back for something else. And if you stick to your intention and achieve your goal, your self-esteem won't fall through the floor just because you didn't get that hottie into bed on the first try. You will have made yourself known, laid some groundwork, and maintained your dignity. And what did everyone think of you? Most likely they thought that you were quite confident. And if not, screw 'em, you achieved your goal for the day.

TEN THINGS THAT CAN SERIOUSLY UNDERMINE YOUR CONFIDENCE:

Feeling gassy

Cold sores

Bad lighting

A sunburn

Panic attacks

Pinkeye

Hiccups

Hat hair

Diarrhea

Boos

Common Traits of Confident People

FROM MOVIE STARS TO CEOS, THERE ARE CERTAIN UNDENIABLE TRUISMS THAT ALL OF LIFE'S WINNERS SHARE. TAKE A LOOK AT THE RULES OF SUCCESS. YOU'LL SEE THAT THEY CAN BE EASILY APPLIED TO YOUR EVERYDAY LIFE:

ASSUME THAT SUCCESS IS POSSIBLE: Do not waste your energy wondering why. Ask yourself, why not?

KNOW WHAT YOU WANT: A clear picture of where you want to go will ensure confidence when you are making decisions about how to get there.

FINISH WHAT YOU START: The world is littered with unfinished screenplays, half-baked business plans, and abandoned dreams. A finished work, no matter how crappy, is always better than an unfinished one, and the mere act of following through builds confidence.

AVOID COMPARING YOURSELF TO OTHERS: There will always be greater and lesser persons than yourself, so measure your own successes on their individual merit. Comparison with others only results in temporary ego swells or sudden plunges in self-esteem.

PUT YOURSELF FIRST: This does not mean screwing over the loved ones, but do not be shy about making your own goals a top priority. If you don't take them seriously, no one else will.

FOCUS ON THE BIGGER PICTURE: If you feel overwhelmed by a challenge, remember that it is no more than one of many stepping-stones on the path to success, and a great deal of pressure will be relieved. Keep each step in perspective.

SPEAK SLOWLY: You will be better heard and better understood if you speak slowly and deliberately. Never rush through anything that matters.

ASK QUESTIONS: Not asking questions for fear of appearing ignorant will only keep you in a state of ignorance. Remember the Chinese proverb:

TEN THINGS THAT CAN BOOST YOUR CONFIDENCE:

Good shoes

A stiff drink

Sexy underwear

Breath mints

An expensive haircut

A killer outfit

A tight ass

An entourage

Good lighting

Success

"He who asks is a fool for five minutes, but he who does not ask remains a fool forever."

The thing always happens that you really believe in; and the belief in a thing makes it happen.
–Frank Lloyd Wright

KEEP YOUR EYES OPEN TO OPPORTUNITIES: If you have no expectation of succeeding, you will be blind to opportunities. Trust that they are there; look for them, and they will appear.

KNOW YOUR OWN PATTERNS: Do you always have a period of writer's block when beginning a new project? Do you usually experience a wave of insecurity in a new relationship? Is there always a phase of panic when you make a life change? If you know your patterns, you will experience less anxiety because you recognize the emotions and you know that they always pass.

ACCEPT THE INEVITABILITY OF REJECTION: Nobody likes it, but no one can escape it. You cannot expect to succeed if you crumble every time you encounter a roadblock. You may decide to give up after ten galleries have rejected your paintings and never realize that the eleventh one would have accepted them. If you stop trying, then your failure is your own fault.

REJECT MAGICAL THINKING: To simply wish to be rich and famous is both vague and dumb. By focusing on realistic and attainable goals, you may eventually get there, but to dream of magical results with no realistic plans will lead nowhere.

TAKE RESPONSIBILITY FOR YOUR SUCCESSES AND YOUR FAILURES: The surest way to lose your power is to write off your successes as lucky flukes or to blame others when things don't go your way. Remain in the driver's seat and you will remain in control.

IF YOU BELIEVE IT, THEY'LL BELIEVE IT: Do not sit around waiting for someone else to proclaim you talented or worthy. The truth is that the perceptions of others are often formed by the cues you are sending.

The Ugliness of Neediness

If there is one thing all true stars avoid like the plague, it is the very notion of appearing needy. Vulnerable? Fine. Sensitive? Sure, why not? Shy? That can work. But the one character trait that is universally unappealing and the antithesis of confidence is neediness. In a nutshell, if you need to be liked, you're in deep doo-doo. Everyone wants to be liked and appreciated, but no one can win everyone over (except you, you sexy magnet!), so the occasional cold shoulder shouldn't bother you any more than a bad smell on the sidewalk. Just keep moving.

Desperation always shows, and a clingy, insecure personality appeals to no one but con artists, scammers, and players. For them, a needy soul is a sitting duck. It's tricky business, because in a romantic situation your intention may be to play shy or coy. Sometimes it pays in interviews to come across humbly when discussing your fantastic accomplishments, but shyness and humility are very different from neediness. Make no mistake about it. The need to be liked, if publicly expressed, will haunt you for the rest of your life. Just ask Sally Field.

Fearlessness

Everyone experiences fear. It is a natural biological reaction to perceived danger. It's what gives you the adrenaline to run from a seriously dangerous situation or lift a car off a loved one who is trapped beneath. But when it comes to smaller psychological fears such as looking foolish or the possibility of failure, the thing that sets winners apart is that they act in the face of their fears.

Those who dream by day are cognizant of many things which escape those who dream only by night.
–Edgar Allan Poe

Countless are the tales of athletes, actors, and business tycoons who report butterflies, nausea, or even the occasional upchuck before stepping into their respective arenas. Of course, you never want to let anyone see you lose your lunch, but it may happen all the same. The thing to keep in mind is that you are not the first person to experience fear or anxiety. The more intense the spotlight, the greater the anxiety. But each time you take to that karaoke stage, present a plan in the conference room, or approach the person that intimidates you at a social function, you are experiencing a little victory.

NO, I COULDN'T POSSIBLY …
According to the American Psychiatric Association, the most common social phobia among adults is the fear of speaking in public.

You may think you are keeping yourself safe from humiliation or failure by avoiding those things you would love to do but are afraid to try. You may think that your fear is the voice of reason. You may convince yourself that it is better to avoid the risk. But every time you decide not to act, you are in fact making a decision. And if that decision involves something that you truly want, every time you decide not to act, you are failing.

The irony is that it appears to be insecurity that is preventing you from trying. In fact, it may very well be a form of egomania. It is very egotistical to believe that everyone is expecting you to be perfect. To think that everyone is watching and waiting to evaluate you and your every endeavor is laughably self-centered. They don't care. Sure, if you're surrounded by mean-spirited people, they may laugh and point, but once you're out of junior high, you really shouldn't be making life decisions based on those idiots.

It is highly unlikely that you will ever succeed if you aren't willing to take a chance and accept the fact that there will be ups and downs.

Donald Trump has faced bankruptcy more than once, and he may very well again someday. People laughed when Cher's name appeared after Meryl Streep's in the opening credits for *Silkwood*. And after some personal challenges, having once been ranked number one in the world, a horrendous losing streak caused Andre Agassi's ranking to drop to an all-time low of 141. Trump came back, Cher won an Oscar, and Agassi got back to number one. Why? Because they refused to accept defeat. And were they scared? I'm guessing yes.

Failure is unimportant. It takes courage to make a fool of yourself.
—Charlie Chaplin

Failing is part of succeeding. Fear and doubt are as inevitable as exhilaration and joy. But only for those who try. Those who refuse to play the game unless they know they can win, never win.

A Cool Head

Any great champion will tell you that you should never let your opponent see you sweat. In business deals, sporting matches, or legal negotiations, the ability to maintain your composure and keep your cool when things are falling apart is essential. The tennis player who throws his racket and screams in disgust is letting his opponent see that he is dissolving. It gives the opponent a rise in confidence because they can see that a meltdown may be imminent. Even when you're losing, you need to act as if you're winning, or at least only temporarily distracted.

Nothing good can ever come from tantrums and emotional breakdowns. Yes, a little anger may fuel the fire temporarily, but you will always be in a precarious position if you are on the brink of an emotional crack-up. If your personality is such that you are prone to hysterical displays, you may never be able to fully contain them, but you had better learn how to keep them in check. Emotional basket cases do not garner much respect. And, yes, there are examples of high-strung, screaming maniacs who have reached high positions, but they are invariably loathed by coworkers and are therefore very vulnerable to the slings and arrows of spite. And that is no way to go through life.

Beyond appearances, and in spite of how you feel inside, keeping your composure in times of great stress actually empowers you. By maintaining a calm and confident demeanor, free of defensiveness and anger, you will actually retain a mental edge that may ultimately lead you to prevail. Your emotions are not random. They are a result of your thoughts. If you can control your thoughts, you can control your emotions, so:

DO remember that the more emotional you become, the less control you have.

DON'T relinquish your power by resorting to tantrums.

DO keep your mouth shut and speak carefully if your anger is rising.

DON'T unleash a verbal tirade for which you may have to apologize later.

DO wait several hours and reread any angry e-mails, letters, or written statements before sending.

DON'T give them evidence of your irrational hysteria in print.

Famous Late Bloomers

Not everyone is lucky enough to come from a background of loving support and encouragement. But a shaky start can always be shaken off. Consider these historical giants who faced significant obstacles on their path to greatness.

Even if you're on the right track, you'll get run over if you just sit there.
—Will Rogers

BEETHOVEN: Despite a tyrannical father who regularly informed him that he was hopeless, little Ludwig went on to become one of the world's most famous composers of all time.

WINSTON CHURCHILL: He failed the sixth grade, slept late, and had a brief flirtation with opium in college, but he still went on to become the prime minister of England.

THOMAS EDISON: Told by a teacher that he was unable to learn, the questionable student went on to invent the light bulb, among many other clever gizmos.

ALBERT EINSTEIN: He was fat and violent, he didn't speak until the age of four, and he couldn't read until the age of seven. Even so, he formulated the theory of relativity.

HENRY FORD: During his teenage years, a formal evaluation declared that he showed "no promise." Still, he managed to form a rather profitable company.

LOUIS PASTEUR: At the École Normale Supérieure in Paris, Pasteur was given a "mediocre" rating in chemistry by a professor. He went on to invent the process of pasteurization and produce the first vaccine for rabies.

ISAAC NEWTON: Newton's early performance in elementary school was evaluated as "poor." So he sulked under a tree and discovered the law of gravity.

The Ultimate Poison

After all is said and done on the subject of confidence, there is one related area that is undeniably a factor in the way we see the world, the things that happen to us, and the amount of "luck" that comes our way. A simple fact of the universe, string theory and all, is that positive energy attracts positive energy, and negative energy attracts the same. There is nothing so poisonous, so self-defeating, and so destructive as a bad attitude.

If you believe that things will go wrong, they will. Is everything hard for you? Is everyone else an idiot? Does everyone screw you over? If so, you are leading quite an extraordinary life! Wow. So much crap all directed at you. What are the odds? Now don't get all twisted on me, but couldn't this have something to do with your expectations?

If, at your very core, there is a belief that life is unfair and things never work out for you, you will be far more likely to watch as things go wrong and will actually allow the tide to turn against you so that you can be proven right. It's a self-fulfilling prophecy. In order to support your life-is-shit theory, you will actually gravitate toward those courses of action, or inaction as the case may be, that will ultimately prove you right. Congratulations.

Sometimes, the instinct for self-protection overrides all else and a person can actually become comfortable in a place of failure. Why?

Because it's easier to expect the worst than to face disappointment. This is one of life's tricky little traps. At some point, every child believes that he or she is special and that anything is possible. Over time, this belief is tested, challenged, even pummeled into the ground, but it is never irretrievable. Every day we have a choice regarding what we choose to focus on. The things we focus on form our core beliefs. And our core beliefs inform every choice we make and everything we do.

If you like, you can spend years and hundreds of thousands of dollars in therapy, but consider this: When you were young and vulnerable, you were at the mercy of those around you. You may have been treated unfairly, or even criminally. But at some point, you must decide to retake control of your life. You must decide what you want. It may be a better job, it may be a trip to Europe, it may be a loving relationship, or it may be a fantastic career. But until you admit that you want it, you deserve it, and it is possible, it won't happen.

See yourself in the setting you desire and think of how it will feel. Let go of the fear, let go of the need for someone else to save you, and decide what you want. Know that there will be bumps in the road, and it may take some time. But if you know who you want to become, you can become that person.

(You see how I almost lost the others completely? So close to sheer corniness, I was. It was a gamble, but I was confident in my argument. Of course, you were with me the entire time, you savvy devil!)

CHAPTER 4

CHARM, CHARISMA, AND STAR QUALITY

If you cannot convince them, confuse them.

—HARRY S. TRUMAN

The "It" Factor

Most people know "it" when they see it, but very few can accurately describe it. Ever since the term was coined in the golden age of Hollywood to describe the silent-screen star Clara Bow, the idea of "it" has been tossed around by casting directors, producers, and movie reviewers with great authority, though its true makeup has never entirely been agreed upon.

However, when asked about the endless parade of actors that pass through their doors, casting directors and modeling agents always agree that you can spot "it" the moment a potential star walks in the room.

Every person carries an aura or a halo of energy that radiates outward and can be felt by others. Even babies and animals react to the energy they pick up from strangers, but the question is whether that energy engages people emotionally or not. Intellect rarely comes into play when it comes to such matters, because "it" is something you feel rather than see. Consider a person standing onstage addressing an audience. If the speaker is thoughtful, reasoning, and intellectual but without magnetism, the audience will quickly lose interest and begin to feel the symptoms of an oncoming coma. But a speaker who can elicit any kind of feeling from an audience, whether it is laughter, sympathy, curiosity, or a rush of blood to the naughty bits, can hold on to the attention and woo the unsuspecting onto their side.

What was once a term that applied only to show business is now something that is appreciated and even sought out by corporate head hunters, political consultants, and even the average human resources department at work. Qualifications, ambition, and dedication are still required, but many studies have shown that when equally qualified candidates apply for the same job, the more charismatic and attractive candidate almost always wins out. And while such blatant superficiality might seem quite discouraging, it is important to note that "attractiveness" is not only about bone structure and good hair. In any scenario, attractiveness is also measured by charm, self-confidence, and demeanor.

For those who are skeptical about such things, consider the fact that in 1993 the Massachusetts Institute of Technology incorporated a charm school into its curriculum. While the school's graduates were universally perceived to be among the cream of the intellectual crop, they often shuffled into interviews with their eyes on the floor, their speech mumbled, and a general appearance that was, shall we say, less than marketable. And while these things may seem unimportant, corporations that spend billions of dollars on marketing, and that rely heavily on the forging of social and business relations, began to realize the importance of social skills. Next thing you know, the students of MIT are taking speech lessons, correcting their droopy deportment, studying etiquette, learning ballroom dancing, and even working the runway in the annual fashion show. (You would think someone would have realized the potential for ticket sales to a show like that.)

Is this all a bit absurd? Well, yes and no. In the end, it's what you do that matters. But if you can represent the company (or yourself) in a positive and effective way, if you can charm partners, strike deals, and make those sales rise in whatever way is effective, then you become a very valuable commodity. It's true for movie stars and it's true for you. After all, who's going to buy cologne from a disheveled, morose scent-spritzer at Bloomies?

The three key elements of the elusive "it" quality are charm, charisma, and star quality. Charm is not the same thing as charisma, which in turn is different from star quality. But when all three are combined in one package, that's when you've undeniably got "it."

What Is Charm?

Of the three elements, charm is perhaps the most attainable by the average person. That is because it is an effect created by behavior. To charm is to actively seduce. It is the result of actions that put others at ease, create a feeling of intimacy, and bring humor and warmth into an otherwise ordinary situation. It is the difference between talking to someone and talking into them. It is about making connections and eliciting positive feelings.

Think about someone you consider extremely charming. Are they witty, approachable, thoughtful, and flirtatious? Probably they are. Are they aloof, distant, and sealed off? Not likely. The essence of charm is warmth. It is achieved first and foremost by paying attention to others, focusing on their mood, and zeroing in on common ground. Really, it's little more than good manners. Joking with the receptionist, smiling at the cashier, or chatting up the guest who is standing alone is a kind and thoughtful thing to do.

Only the most surly of characters will not respond well to attention. Whether you're applying for a job, meeting the potential in-laws, or just floating around a cocktail party, you will make a much better impression and register in the minds of others if you make an effort. Just because Grandma is old and seems a bit disgruntled doesn't mean she won't appreciate a little flirtation and a dash of racy humor. Most likely she's bored and grumpy because everyone is treating her as if she's made of glass. And in the workplace, that

It is absurd to divide people into good and bad. People are either charming or tedious.
—Oscar Wilde

intimidating executive is far more likely to be impressed by you if you manage to connect through a little humor or social observation than by shamelessly and nervously sucking up and boring him or her to death with your tedious work babble.

The golden rule of charm is the most basic rule of human decency: Treat everyone as if they matter. Make a deliberate connection. Don't try to become everyone's best friend. That's not the goal. Just show an interest and take the focus off yourself. You'll find that in addition to being highly effective, it's a huge relief, socially speaking. It's much easier to ask a few questions than spend the entire evening exhaustively trying to sell yourself to everyone. Here are some easy guidelines to keep in mind.

Look the other person in the eye, even if it's for short intervals. It shows confidence and a willingness to connect. Stare at the floor, and you've lost them.

Flattery goes a long way, but lies are always transparent. If your host's outfit is hideous, compliment her on the party's turnout. If the receptionist has a gruesome cold sore, compliment him on his shoes.

Flirtation is fun, but overt sexuality can be threatening. A quick wink is always better than a long, leering look.

By focusing on the other person, you will experience less insecurity as to how interesting you are. Find out what they're thinking and look for common ground.

Don't overdo it. If you feel you are forcing it, you probably are. If the situation isn't going well, just excuse yourself with a knowing smile.

Never linger too long. Stick to the old show biz ideal of leaving them wanting more. Trust that if romance or friendship is looming, you'll gravitate back to one another.

Let the other person feel that they have made the social affair more fun for you. The goal is to leave them feeling good about themselves, not you. They should feel as if *they* have charmed *you*.

THE BETTER YOU BECOME AT CHARMING PEOPLE, THE SMOOTHER THINGS WILL GO FOR YOU IN EVERY ASPECT OF LIFE. BUT BEYOND POTENTIAL EMPLOYERS AND ROMANTIC PROSPECTS, IT IS IMPORTANT TO ISOLATE AND TARGET THOSE FROM WHOM YOUR CHARMS MAY ELICIT THE GREATEST REWARDS ON AN EVERYDAY BASIS:

TEN WORTHY CHARM TARGETS:

Bartenders	*Accountants*
Receptionists	*Juries*
Flight attendants	*Creditors*
In-laws	*Your lover's dog*
Landlords	*Anyone who intimidates you*

What Is Charisma?

Unlike charm, charisma has more to do with innate magnetism and leadership qualities that tend to impress groups more than individuals. However, that doesn't mean that one cannot cultivate charisma. And while charm is fairly benign, charisma can be used for both good and evil. History has shown that leaders of cults, religions, and even entire nations can bring about catastrophic tragedy when followers trust blindly in what they see and perceive. Charisma may manifest itself as self-confidence, sexual electricity, inspirational magnetism, or even political power. It is the most volatile of the three elements, and it is therefore the most powerful, because people tend to project what they want to see onto a charismatic personality, even if it conflicts with what that person is actually doing or saying.

Life engenders life. Energy creates energy. It is by spending oneself that one becomes rich.
—Sarah Bernhardt

In its most innocent form, charisma can create feelings of devotion and trust in an audience of any kind. A great speaker who is both empathetic and passionate can stir up great emotion in a group. A comedian can generate huge laughs by tapping into the audience's anger or sympathy. And a sense of danger, sexual threat, or edginess can make a person seem thrilling and eminently watchable. In any case, it's all about electricity. Charisma doesn't have to be dangerous, but it always involves an emotional response in people, and that is why a charismatic politician can sway the masses, despite questionable policies. Even those we dislike may be able to influence us with their undeniable ability to command attention.

Interestingly, those who exude the greatest charisma often seem to produce very mixed feelings in their audiences. The stronger the emotion, the stronger the reaction. Charisma is subjective, so what appeals to some may turn others off. But regardless of interpretation, true charisma rattles the cages of everyone, one way or another. Think of Bill Clinton, Martha Stewart, or Ronald Reagan. People tend to love them or hate them. And of course, there are far more sinister examples one can point to. However, it should be clear by now that in this lighthearted exposé we want to embrace the positive aspects of charisma and use them for the greater good.

SO, WHAT IS IT, EXACTLY? IT IS THE ABILITY TO COMMAND ATTENTION, THE ABILITY TO DISTRACT, AND THE ABILITY TO CAPTIVATE AN AUDIENCE VIA FOUR DIFFERENT MEANS:

PRESENCE: Your personal style, posture, and body language should command attention. You may be impeccably controlled or outlandishly unpredictable, but never invisible.

MANNER: Natural ease and grace make you believable and worthy of respect. Effortless humor and relaxed confidence are far more effective than polite pretense or forced intensity.

MYSTERY: By never revealing everything, you create curiosity and fascination. Surprise them with the unexpected and make them believe they are learning secrets.

EMPATHY: The ability to connect emotionally as well as intellectually creates trust. Let your audience know that you're on their side, and they'll be on yours.

Countless studies have shown that most people form an impression of a person within ten seconds of their entering a room, taking to the stage, or appearing on-screen. This impression is based on the four building blocks of charisma mentioned above. In short, your belief in yourself and your belief in your mission can actually eclipse your credibility. Now, in regard to political tyrants, this is bad news. In the case of personal self-advancement, it's good news.

Granted, the tests of charisma are a bit trickier than charming Grandma at a wedding, but really there's no reason to employ charisma if you don't have a purpose, unless you're simply starved for a little attention. But the purpose is always relative. Maybe you just want to drum up business. Maybe you're selling yourself to a prospective employer. Or maybe you just want to get the bridesmaids at a wedding to head to the hotel bar. The keys are to have an intention, a purpose, and a true belief that all will benefit from your singular vision. Think of yourself as an usher with the only flashlight in the house, and you're halfway there. Then ask yourself:

CAN YOU LIVEN UP A DULL PARTY?

CAN YOU READ THE EMOTIONAL TONE OF A CROWD?

ARE YOU EMOTIONALLY EXPRESSIVE?

ARE YOU FUNNY?

ARE YOU ABLE TO USE YOUR VOCAL TONE TO YOUR ADVANTAGE?

ARE YOU ABLE TO CONVEY ENTHUSIASM?

ARE YOU ABLE TO COMMUNICATE IDEAS CLEARLY?

DO YOU HAVE A VISION FOR IMPROVING THE CIRCUMSTANCE AT HAND?

DO YOU BELIEVE IN WHAT YOU ARE SAYING?

ARE YOU CONFIDENT IN YOUR ABILITY TO PERSUADE?

The word *charisma* is derived from the ancient Greek *charis,* which means a certain grace or gift. The idea is that the gods have breathed a special spirit into you. Nice, huh? It all boils down to a belief that you are unique and powerful, which you certainly are, you big throbbing magnet, you. Look at you, oozing charisma all over these pages. Get a napkin!

TEN SIGNS THAT YOU'RE RADIATING:

STRANGERS ASK YOU FOR DIRECTIONS.

HEADS TURN WHEN YOU ENTER A ROOM.

OTHERS OFFER TO PICK UP THE CHECK.

PEOPLE GIVE WAY TO YOU ON THE SIDEWALK.

YOU GET INVITED TO SOIREES YOU WOULD NEVER ATTEND.

CASUAL ACQUAINTANCES ASK FOR ADVICE.

YOU GET INCREASED OPPORTUNITIES FOR NONCOMMITTAL SEX.

STRANGERS ASK YOU WHERE YOU GOT YOUR JEANS.

YOU CATCH PEOPLE STARING AT YOU.

MONEY STARTS FALLING FROM THE SKY.

Star Quality

All right, we now come to the most indefinable of the three elements —the mystical and elusive "star quality." Truth be told, any forthcoming casting director will tell you that it's all about fuckability. Crass perhaps, but undeniable. There is simply no denying that sexual appeal has a profound effect on how people perceive and respond to us. Even if they are unaware of their subconscious desires, people will always give the benefit of the doubt, lend a helping hand, and seek to help those to whom they are attracted. Now, it is important to point out here that this is not a recommendation to engage in careless promiscuity, general sluttiness, or the shameless use of a trick jaw. These things may get you dinner, but they will never get you respect.

The nice thing about being a celebrity is that, if you bore people, they think it's their fault.
—Henry Kissinger

True sex appeal, the kind that makes people do crazy things on your behalf, is rooted in the ever-alluring promise of "maybe." No great plays were ever written about anyone who puts out in the first act. Desire and pursuit are far more dizzying than an easy lay. Sexual promise and emotional mystery have made cinematic superstars out of ordinary mortals. It is the possibility of sex that makes both men and women fixate. Once again, the measure is in the perception of others. If you can suggest a possibility, you can create a fascination.

Sex appeal, as a raw element, translates very well on film. In the workplace or in social situations, subtlety behooves the sexy. Overt efforts are usually transparent and can result in troublesome trips to the HR office, but a subtle availability can do wonders. The greatest stars are those who somehow make us believe that if we could only penetrate their rarefied orbit and tap into their vulnerable sensitivity, well, then they'd fall for us hook, line, and sinker. Keep that in mind.

For those who prefer to be the pursuer rather than the pursued, successful seduction still requires an element of vulnerability and self-revelation. Few people dream of being seduced by a bulldozer, but when confidence is combined with an endearing playfulness, well, then you've got something. In any case, you need to know whether you are playing the pursuer or the pursued. Which is best suited to the archetype(s) you embody? Make sure you're clear on that. If you're not, please revisit Chapter 1 for clarification.

Lest it be concluded that star quality is solely about sex, it is important to point out that wit, wisdom, and insight are wildly appealing qualities in our celluloid icons, in our political leaders, and in our coworkers. Therefore, it follows that humor, personality, humanity, and accessibility are very endearing traits in the real world as well. Your aloof attitude may protect you from emotional entanglement, but it will get you nowhere when it comes to life experience. You don't need to be reckless, but star quality demands that you admit to your humanity. No one has ever fallen in love with an ice cube.

So, whereas charm and charisma are primarily based on the effect you produce on others, star quality is defined by the degree to which you allow yourself to be seen. Small glimpses into the heart—or down the blouse—of a person allow us to observe the soul behind the physical presence. And it is those little glimpses that make us fall in love. Of course, there is a limit to all things, and in matters such as these, small hints and little doses are best.

WHEN IT COMES TO CULTIVATING ONE'S OWN STAR QUALITY, THERE ARE CERTAIN TRUTHS, PRACTICES, AND NUGGETS OF ADVICE TO KEEP IN MIND:

Work hard to free yourself of bitterness and negativity. You will never shine with such dark baggage, and if you cling to it, you'll only get more of the same.

Remain relaxed in social situations. Charm, charisma, and star quality must never be forced. It is better to improve slowly than to try too hard.

Study the behaviors and body language of others you believe have star quality, and experiment with those behaviors.

Pay attention to the energy that comes with attraction, flirtation, and seduction. Become familiar with the feeling and you will eventually be able to create that feeling.

Ask yourself what kind of person you would like to be if you had no fears or insecurities. Keep that ideal in mind and work toward becoming that person.

As Leroy "Satchel" Paige once said, "Work like you don't need the money, love like you've never been hurt, dance like there's nobody watching."

Vanity, Arrogance, and Conceit

Charming as you are, it is highly unlikely that you would ever drift into offenses such as these. Even so, there are a great many people who seem to have difficulty identifying where charm, charisma, and star quality end, and vanity, arrogance, and conceit begin. But it's really quite simple.

Vanity begins at the point where your focus on others is replaced by a focus entirely on yourself. Charming people do not need to be flattered or validated. It is perfectly reasonable to enjoy attention, but to rely on appearance alone is not very attractive.

Arrogance is an abrasive, overbearing confidence. It is one thing to feel confident that you are at your best, but it is another thing entirely to succumb to the delusion that you are superior to others. Such transparent obnoxiousness will only isolate you.

Conceit is generally defined as an excess of pride. Smugness and gloating are two of the quickest and surest ways to turn others off. A healthy sense of self-esteem is essential for anyone who hopes to succeed in life, but leave the admiration and awe to your audience.

Pulling Focus and Harnessing the Spotlight

You do realize, of course, that endeavors such as these require discretion and tact? Pulling focus is one thing, but stealing someone else's thunder is unkind. Harnessing the spotlight is perfectly reasonable, but hogging the spotlight is unseemly. As in all things, caution and sensitivity are essential as you humbly maneuver your way toward the center of the stage. But you knew that.

So, now that we've established that charm is about humility, charisma requires responsibility, and star quality is enhanced by a degree of vulnerability, it's time to ratchet things up, have a little fun, and kick some ass. Subtlety is all well and good, but if true fame is ever going to be achieved, and if you're going to make use

As one goes through life one learns that if you don't paddle your own canoe, you don't move.

–Katharine Hepburn

of your natural gifts, you'll need to tap into your inner keg of shamelessness. Just remember to keep the nozzle on "gentle spray" rather than "jet stream."

It is best to experiment incrementally in the work-a-day world, but when true opportunities to shine arise, you must be able to kick into a higher gear. There is a time and place for your sensitive inner child, and then there are those moments when the spotlight beckons, the heat increases, and you simply have to step up to the plate. Your personal "star moment" may arise at any time, in any one of a million scenarios. But when those rare windows of opportunity present themselves, you'll know it, and those are the times when you just have to jump out of the plane:

REJECT NERVOUSNESS, AND SEE IT AS EXCITEMENT.

REMEMBER THAT THIS IS WHAT YOU USED TO DREAM OF.

TRUST YOURSELF.

PUSH AHEAD NO MATTER WHAT.

GIVE GOOD CHARM.

GIVE YOUR INSECURITIES THE NIGHT OFF.

ENJOY THE HIGH OF THE ENERGY AND ELECTRICITY.

You'll be fine as long as you enjoy it, own it, and stay true to yourself. You don't need to pretend to be anyone other than yourself. A rebel will rebel, a flirt will flirt, and you will do what you do. Just do it well. After all, you know who you are by now, and there is no pretense here. You know that your greatest strength lies in simply being your indisputably original self, right? We covered that, didn't we? Heh? No? Oh. Well, then I take full responsibility for this charming faux pas, and I invite you to turn the page.

CHAPTER 5

INDIVIDUALITY

Cherish forever what makes you unique, 'cuz you're really a yawn if it goes.

—BETTE MIDLER

A Copy Is Just a Copy

Amid all this conversation of playing the fame game, understanding the importance of first impressions and adherence to rules, it is essential to point out that there is nothing so important as individuality. Though it may seem contradictory to all that has been heretofore discussed, individuality is the key to emerging as a star in your world, be it global or local.

Remember that an archetype is a loose definition at best, and your job is to make that archetype entirely your own. Stealing tricks and following role models is one thing, but if you don't know what sets you apart, you'd better start thinking about it. It's essential to identify that which makes you unlike any other in order to separate yourself from the masses. After all, no one ever rose to stardom by being supremely average.

Modeling oneself detail for detail after a celebrity is a recipe for failure. No matter how effective you may be in your imitation, you will never be more than that—an imitation. In order to rise up into the rarefied realm of celebulosity, you need to identify and embrace your imperfections and turn them into assets. In the face of societal pressure to conform and the quick fixes offered by plastic surgery, it is essential to maintain a healthy respect for the one-of-a-kind genetic wonder that you are.

In a cookie-cutter society, there is tremendous pressure to imitate and emulate others who have succeeded. However, if you find yourself looking to others as role models, or even worse as physical models, you may be tragically undermining yourself. It is absolutely essential to understand that there is no one else like you on the planet. Your voice, your style, your viewpoint, your humor, your talent, and your appearance are your greatest assets. So don't try to diminish them.

The greatest crime you can commit against the laws of the universe is to homogenize yourself. Unless your goal is to disappear completely, you need to resist the temptation to assuage your insecurities by eliminating the very things that make you stand out. Trust me, there's this chick in England who spent hundreds of thousands of dollars on countless surgeries so that she could look exactly like a Barbie doll. She got her wish and she got on the news, but really, how is that life going to turn out?

Don't compromise yourself. You are all you've got.
– Janis Joplin

BEHOLD THE STARS WHO HELD THEIR GROUND, WHERE LESSER MORTALS MAY HAVE BEEN TEMPTED TO TAMPER WITH THEIR IMPERFECTIONS:

THE GAP-TOOTH GRIN:
Madonna, David Letterman, Lauren Hutton

THE BIG SCHNOZZ:
Adrian Brody, Barbra Streisand, Rossi de Palma

THE BIG BACKYARD:
Jennifer Lopez, Anna Nicole Smith, Aretha Franklin

THE LANTERN JAW:
Jay Leno, Celine Dion, Ben Affleck

DROOPY EYES:
Bette Davis, Benicio del Toro, Al Pacino

RECEDING HAIRLINES:
Sting, Jack Nicholson, Ed Harris

GRAY HAIR:
George Clooney, Richard Gere, Lily Munster

Iconography

Throughout the ages and still today, there have always been
cultures that eschew or even forbid the worship of icons. The
Western world sees things quite differently. From corporate logos
to still photographs of the celebrities we worship, iconography is
big business, and to make an imprint is to establish a brand that can
last a very long time. Consider the following images:

**A BLONDE WOMAN ON A SUBWAY GRATING WITH HER WHITE
DRESS BEING BLOWN UPWARD**

**A SLUMPED FIGURE IN A RED WINDBREAKER, JEANS, AND A
BLOND DA (OR DUCK'S ASS HAIRDO)**

A LONG-HAIRED WOMAN STANDING READY IN A FUR BIKINI

**A MALE SINGER WITH LONG SIDEBURNS, IN A WHITE JUMPSUIT,
SURROUNDED BY VEGAS LIGHTS**

**A LONE FIGURE IN A TRAMP'S SUIT WITH A CANE AND A BOW-
LER HAT**

**A DISCO DANCER, ONE ARM RAISED, IN A WHITE SUIT ON A
FLOOR OF LIGHTS**

Chances are you can identify the celebrity with whom each of these
images is connected. A single photograph or a movie still can make
a career, for better or worse, when an iconic image is created and
seared into the public consciousness. But the reason these images
are so identifiable is not based entirely on the clothing and hair,
though they are essential elements. The body language or the pose

of the subject also plays a major part in the equation. It's Marilyn's legs set apart and the look of ecstasy on her face, James Dean's burdened posture and troubled expression, Raquel Welch's heightened sense of sexual danger. Consider Elvis pointing to the side, Charlie Chaplin's turned out feet, or John Travolta's famous pose, so often and unnecessarily emulated at drunken weddings.

The overriding theme here is that it's not just fashion, it's not just physicality, and it's not just a pose. An iconic image is created when all of the elements work together in perfect harmony. Each element reflects the others. Now, in the day-to-day world, it would be unwise to don a costume, strike a pose, and hope a photographer shows up, but if you consider the idea of movement, style, and attitude working in harmony, you can apply that idea to your own sense of style and thereby enhance your own individuality.

So, if you consider yourself a rebel/fashionista/flirt who wants to convey both power and an ironic sense of humor, think Gwen Stefani. An outsider/player/heartthrob conveying a bit of edge and sense of mystery might be Colin Farrell. You get the idea. Your style, your attitude, and your movement all play a part in the overall impact of the image you project, and the greater the harmony, the stronger and more cohesive that image becomes.

But once again, you need to develop your own identity, and that identity can and should evolve and change over time, just as you and your personality evolve and change. You may have your trademark glasses, your signature style, or your highly complicated goatee, but the last thing you want is to become frozen in time.

There is no excellent beauty that hath not some strangeness in the proportion.
—Sir Francis Bacon

Yes, I know that you would never allow yourself to become frozen in time. You are far too shrewd and self-aware for that. And I also appreciate your sense of understatement. Really, that's one of the things I admire most about you. You know that you don't need to try too hard, and you understand that a little bit can go a long way. Nonetheless, you can't deny that you, too, could do a little more to hone your style and maybe even add a bit of flash. I mean let's be honest here. You're good, but you could do better.

In any case, the lesson here is that you'll never make much of an impact if you send mixed or diluted messages. You don't need to wake up every day and calculate the powerful signals you'll be sending, but it never hurts to have a strong sense of who you are and how you'd like to be perceived. Keep it in the back of your mind, and the day-to-day choices you make will start to become more and more cohesive, and in turn you will begin to make a stronger impression on people. And the stronger and more consistent your image, the more memorable as an individual you will become.

Fashion Infamy

At the 2001 Academy Awards, the Icelandic pop star Bjork performed her haunting song "I've Seen It All," which was nominated for an award in the category of Best Original Song. Her performance was both edgy and sublime, but very few people remember it today. What they do recall, and probably always will, is her bizarre outfit, which took the form of a dead swan draped around her body, complete with a billed head and white tutu.

Her song may not have taken home the prize, but she did secure a spot on virtually every "worst-dressed" list of the year. It was a fantastic example of fashion infamy. When she stepped onto the red carpet, she was far from a household name in the United States, but by the following morning, her picture was splashed across the world, eclipsing the efforts of much larger luminaries. This was not the result of an unfortunate fashion faux pas, but a brilliant use of fashion to both make an irreverent statement and steal the spotlight on the world's grandest stage. I mean, really, how could anyone have missed the humor?

Bjork had two options. She could try to look pretty and glamorous like everyone else at the ceremony, then sing her song and go home, or she could show up in the most absurdly outrageous, but oddly endearing, getup imaginable and command the attention of virtually every media outlet in the world. She made a very wise and highly individual choice. No danger of anyone else showing up in that dress. And though it's true, she may actually have thought she looked kind of cute, it is impossible to believe that she wasn't winking at us all on some level.

NOTORIOUS RED CARPET CRIMES

1986 Cher gives the Academy the finger by arriving dressed as a sequined dominatrix.

1989 Demi Moore designs own disaster with stretchy bicycle shorts and a sequined waist cape.

Remember always that you not only have the right to be an individual, you have an obligation to be one.
—Eleanor Roosevelt

1990 Kim Basinger self-designs silver atrocity featuring a half-jacket and balloon skirt.

1992 Geena Davis opts for an upside-down Kleenex box—mini in front, train in back.

1999 Celine Dion's backward cream tuxedo and fedora look lousy coming and going.

2003 Lara Flynn Boyle is all elbows and knees in a pink tutu and ribbon shoes.

To fly in the face of convention requires both confidence and a playful sense of humor about oneself. But it's a tricky tightrope to walk. Sadly, since the days of punk, new wave, and the '80s Brit-pop invasion have passed, Western society has embarked on a long, dreary slide into extreme conservatism. Unbridled creativity, personal expression, and free-spirited humor are no longer appreciated as they once were. In fact, they now elicit more suspicion and fear than delight and admiration. That said, it is entirely up to you whether you choose to play by the current rules or thumb your nose at the status quo. Happily, there are still a few mavericks out there unafraid to maintain their individual interpretations of beauty and unique style.

ADAMANTLY INDIVIDUAL STAR PEOPLE

Marilyn Manson
A nightmare personified in the minds of conservative parents, old Marilyn is just practicing a little theatre-of-the-macabre. Personally, I always thought KISS was much creepier.

Boy George
From the beginning, the chipper drag queen with the velvety voice was an oddly nonthreatening presence. Ironically, it was only during his brief slide into drug addiction that he stopped dressing up, and that's when he really got scary.

Li'l Kim
Eyelashes, boobs, sequins, and leather straps keep this tiny terror in our faces, but the visuals pale in comparison to her raunchy lyrics. Still, she provides a valuable yardstick, as we all love to debate the measure of vulgarity.

Cher
Once again, the name pops up due to decades of outrageous, belly-baring costumes and gravity-defying headdresses. A true icon of individuality, she has guaranteed that she will never be confused with anyone else.

George Clinton
The grandfather of funk raises eyebrows with Day-Glo dreadlocks and a wardrobe that calls to mind a Las Vegas yard sale. Though his musical contributions may not have always received the acknowledgment they deserve, his presence will never go unnoticed.

GOOD PROP—BAD PROP

NEVER UNDERESTIMATE THE POWER OF A GOOD PROP OR ACCESSORY
TO CONJURE UP A LITTLE PANACHE. OF COURSE, THERE ARE ALSO THOSE
THAT CAN WORK AGAINST YOU. WHETHER YOU'RE ON THE STREET, AT A
PREMIERE, OR DOING BUSINESS, YOU NEED TO KNOW WHICH LOOK
YOU'RE GOING FOR:

Cool	Camp
Sunglasses	Veils
Dog	Cat
Leather	Lace
Motorcycle	Vespa
Cane	Walker
Cigarette case	Cigarette holder
Driving gloves	Colorful mittens
Scarf	Feather boa
Hats	Headdresses

Personal Style

There is something very appealing about imperfection. That's why
the boy heartthrob shows up on the red carpet with a perfect tuxedo
but with slightly disheveled, bed-head hair. That tells us that his
sex appeal is effortless and that maybe he recently had sex. The
screen goddess arrives in an obscenely expensive gown, but she
has carefully crafted runaway curls that give the impression of

easy, unavoidable glamour. She's falling apart but she's still more glamorous than you can ever hope to be.

Just as a hopelessly coordinated and overly designed home has a feeling of sterility, so does a hopelessly coordinated and overly designed person. You are not furniture. If everything is perfect, we lose interest. A "perfect" appearance conjures up uncomfortable images of those disturbing children's beauty pageants. The trick lies in understanding understatement and calculated imperfection. The perfect hairdo always looks better after you've run your fingers through it. An outfit always looks best if it's been properly tailored so that you can move. If the outfit is wearing you, you've lost control of the situation.

SO, REMEMBER TO BE STRONG, TO RESIST THE GENERIC AT ALL COSTS, AND WATCH OUT FOR THESE COMMON PITFALLS:

DO allow your inner eccentric to emerge occasionally.

DON'T choose goofy outfits or weird accessories just to stand out.

DO remember that what seemed really cool at twenty may seem tragic at thirty.

DON'T get a tattoo of your favorite band or the awesome new cult you just joined.

DO accept the aging process and let your style evolve accordingly.

DON'T try to look twenty-five when you're fifty. Your new duck lips won't fool anybody.

DO mix things up and experiment from time to time.

DON'T go against your instincts if you don't think you can pull it off.

DO send me a photograph of your latest hairstyle.

DON'T blame me if it's hideous.

I joke. I have no doubt whatsoever that you'll look fantastic in your new faux-hawk. But still, there is more work to do. The new you has got to get out there and be seen, and if you're going to be seen, we need to have a little discussion about that walk of yours.

CHAPTER 6

BODY
LANGUAGE

There's a fine line between fishing and standing on the shore like an idiot.
—STEVEN WRIGHT

Best in Show

The next time you find yourself watching a major Hollywood awards show, pay close attention to the sight of the publicists shepherding and parading their world-famous clients past a range of looming lenses and skeptical eyes, hoping desperately that they won't misbehave in public. As you take in the grand spectacle, you will note a distinct similarity to the famed

Westminster Kennel Club Show. As the dogs are trotted by the judges, so are the celebrities being keenly evaluated on a variety of "standards." It's eerie, no?

At Westminster, you see, all dogs are divided into seven different "groups." After all, we have different expectations of different groups, n'est-ce pas? This also holds true for celebrities.

THE GROUPS

WORKING *(character actors, indie-film stars)*

TERRIER *(aging actors, diminutive prima donnas)*

TOY *(sexy, nubile, youthful stars on the rise)*

NONSPORTING *(intellectual types, British actors)*

SPORTING *(action-film stars)*

HOUND *(famed womanizers, droopy-eyed has-beens)*

HERDING *(directors, actresses who "accept" mother roles)*

ONCE CORRECTLY CLASSIFIED, THE DOGS ARE JUDGED ON A VARIETY OF STANDARDS.

THE STANDARDS

GENERAL APPEARANCE *(clear enough)*

MOVEMENT *(carriage and willingness to pose for photographers)*

TEMPERAMENT *(congeniality and cooperativeness with the press)*

HEIGHT AND WEIGHT *(overall proportions)*

COAT AND COLOR *(outfit)*

EYE COLOR AND PLACEMENT *(makeup)*

EAR PLACEMENT *(often disguised by hairdo)*

FEET *(shoes)*

TAIL *(not to be underestimated)*

For dogs and celebrities alike, an appearance on television is an invitation to scrutiny. Once your image is transmitted through the airwaves and into the little judgment box, you can be sure that an endless field of couch potatoes is busy at work sizing you up. Unless a crime is involved, people are rarely forced to go on television, so to step in front of a camera is usually a voluntary exercise. If you choose to do so, there's just no getting around the fact that you'll need to pay extra attention to your breeding, grooming, and showmanship. Unless, of course, you have no ambition whatsoever to make it to the second round. Remember that behaving spectacularly and making a spectacle of yourself are very different things. The dog that shits on the judge's shoes may get a big laugh, but there will surely be hell to pay backstage.

Like it or not, if these highly enforced standards of evaluation have already jumped species, well, you don't want to fall behind the dogs. But rather than project our societal neuroses onto our dear four-legged friends, perhaps we should endeavor to evaluate our own physicalities, our movement, and the messages we project on a daily basis.

Posture, Movement, and Carriage

Having established that body type, personal style, and speech are serious considerations in the fame game, we must now look to the area of movement. The ways in which you walk, sit, and present yourself physically to the judges (real or imagined) also play a part in the overall impression you make upon others. A person who shuffles into a room and slumps into a chair isn't going to create a big stir and grab the spotlight. Conversely, someone who glides into a room as if entering onto a grand stage may illicit more chuckles than respect.

The key is really to move with purpose and intention, and to own the space that you are in. A flawless runway walk is not the goal here. In fact, walking itself is not even a requirement. Even in a wheelchair, a commanding sense of self, a strong presence, and assertive body language can be highly effective. I mean really, Jesus entered Jerusalem on a donkey, for God's sake.

That said, it is worth reviewing the most common styles of walking, and examining the messages they send. Like facial expressions and fashion statements, the way we walk says a lot about who we are. Sit on a bench sometime and observe; you'll see. And consider the following variations. Does one of them apply to you?

THE BRAIN ON A STICK: This person is entirely cerebral and unaware of their physicality, galumphing along in deep thought as if the body is no more than a taxi for the head. Usually coupled with a painfully bland wardrobe.

THE LIQUID BALANCER: As if balancing a saucer of milk upon the head, this person walks with barely detectable arm motion and a stubborn refusal to move up and down. It is usually an indication of great self-consciousness and fear of exposure, though sometimes it just means the outfit is far too snug.

THE RUNWAY GLIDE: Hips and shoulders alternate with rhythmic precision as if photos are being taken at every moment. While effective on the catwalk or the red carpet, it often reads as comical on the sidewalk or at the office. Usually a sign of great ambition and/or mild delusion.

THE HITCH-AND-STRUT: Characterized by a rhythmic bounce on the balls of the feet, an upturned chin, and exaggerated arm swing, this mode of personal transport is often seen in shorter people who are subconsciously trying to assert their presence. The up-and-down movement provides the subject with momentary flashes of increased height.

THE PANTHER PROWL: Seen in both women and men. The focus of the movement is in the hips and thighs with fluid arm movement and decreased speed. Usually intended to convey sexual danger, it can veer into comedy when accompanied by too much jewelry or pursed lips.

THE DRUNKEN PUPPET: Slightly off-balance, with frequent head tilts and hands held in front of the body in the manner of a hamster, this unusual variation is often accompanied by sudden starts and stops. Though it may indicate a drinking problem or inner-ear imbalance, more often than not it simply indicates a lack of confidence, hesitancy, and a case of the cutes.

She can make any move, any gesture, almost insufferably suggestive.
–Henry Hathaway on Marilyn Monroe

ATLAS WEAKENING: When carrying the weight of the world on one's shoulders, one tends to droop, over time. Such is the message sent by this martyr-in-transit. Slumping shoulders, a curved back, and a hangdog look tell us that someone's feeling a bit overwhelmed and none too happy.

BIG-BALL STAGGER: Most often seen in athletic men and really butch women, the side-to-side gait is caused by the placement of the feet, not in a straight line, but slightly out to the sides. While the intended message is clear, it can also conjure up unfortunate images of a diaper rash.

THE PIMP DRAG: A curious affectation originating in the inner city, this little performance is intended to suggest two things: a dangerous attitude and discomfort resulting from overwhelming masculinity. It is highly amusing when employed by suburban, white teenage males.

DO-ME-NOW: An arched back, floating arms, and frequent glances over the shoulder send an unseemly message of availability. Ironically, it is almost always employed by the last person on earth you'd want to sleep with.

FALLING FORWARD: Seemingly unique to taller individuals with low self-esteem, the swift, sideways stagger forward with upturned chin seems to suggest ongoing tardiness or implied apology. An ironic and self-defeating waste of physicality, given that height is so often associated with confidence.

THE EMERGENCY QUICKSTEP: Small, quick, panicky steps and an unreasonable impatience with human traffic give the impression that this person is on the way to save the world. Generally speaking, it can be assumed that those exhibiting such a hasty scurry hold the military in high regard and believe that everyone else is an idiot. Not surprisingly, they are often perceived as idiots themselves.

So, what does it all mean? Does everyone have a silly walk? No, but the above examples are not among the most desirable. And how do successful, magnetic people walk? It all comes down to rhythm. Any form of movement is a form of dance and athleticism. And effective movement, like effective communication, has rhythm, tempo, and ease. The trick is to let go of the inhibitions or overcompensations that are making you move unnaturally.

Awareness is essential. Just as you must listen to your voice to rid yourself of awkward speech problems, you must become aware of your body and your movement to seize control of your physicality. If any of the above descriptions rang a bell, you may want to shake out the arms and legs and loosen up. A silly walk is an inhibited or affected walk. If you are self-consciously stiff, recognizing that will help you let go. If you are putting on an act, admit it to yourself and knock it off. If you've never even considered how you walk, then it's time to step it up.

The goal here is not to develop a false or affected movement. The goal is simply to get in touch with your body and allow yourself to move freely, comfortably, and confidently. Because it is those that move with ease and appear to be comfortable within their skins that we find most attractive.

GENERAL RULES FOR A GROOVY GLIDE

STAND UP STRAIGHT

SHOULDERS BACK

RELEASE HIP TENSION

RELEASE KNEE TENSION

ARMS LOOSE

EYES AHEAD

Now, don't be stiff; just keep your archetype and your intention in mind and let them become part of the overall movement. Excellent. Blue ribbon for you.

Beyond the Walk

As always, your physical comfort level is a good indicator of your emotional state. In a job interview, if you sit too far back in a chair, you may seem uninterested or arrogant. Sit on the edge of the chair and you'll look nervous and jumpy. Just sit in the middle and make yourself as comfortable as possible. If you find yourself in the highly energized atmosphere of a television interview, you mustn't let your nerves paralyze you. Don't get caught sitting flat-footed with your hands clutching the armrests as if you're waiting to be electrocuted. Cross your legs, shift your weight to one side, or do whatever it takes to make you feel as if you are in a friend's living room. But get into position before the cameras begin to roll or you'll be fidgeting around like a nervous wreck.

In the conference room, on a date, at a social function, or at an audition, the interpretation by others of your body language is almost exclusively determined by your comfort level. Of course, all this focus may make you a bit self-conscious at first, but once an awareness has been established, you will very quickly begin to find that small adjustments go a long way. If you think about the greatest and most mesmerizing icons of film, music, or even politics, you'll begin to see that beyond beauty, charisma, or even vision and purpose, the confidence or magic we perceive in them is partially rooted in their body language. Whether they are suave and smooth, raw and animalistic, or coy and playful, the body language often speaks louder than the words.

It has been said that up to 90 percent of communication is nonverbal. And while it is difficult to quantify such things, you can be sure that you are sending messages every second of the day. You may think you're sitting in silence, giving nothing away as you listen to that awful coworker of yours proposing a stupid idea, but in fact, your body language may be giving you away. Do you realize the expression you have on your face? Is your body twisted in disapproval? Are you aware of how much you're fidgeting? It pays to keep these things in check.

SIGNS OF ATTRACTION

NOT SURE IF THEY LIKE YOU? LOOK FOR THESE SIGNS:

WHEN MEN ARE ATTRACTED, THEY OFTEN PLAY WITH THEIR EARLOBE.

WHEN WOMEN ARE ATTRACTED, THEY TWIRL A LOCK OF HAIR OR REPEATEDLY TUCK IT BEHIND THE EAR.

IF YOU ARE ATTRACTED TO SOMEONE, WHETHER STANDING OR SEATED, YOUR FEET WILL USUALLY BE POINTED IN THEIR DIRECTION.

SIGNS OF A LIE

A PERSON WILL OFTEN TOUCH THEIR FACE, ESPECIALLY THE NOSE, IMMEDIATELY AFTER LYING.

EYES THAT KEEP LOOKING TO THE RIGHT INDICATE THE CREATIVE SIDE OF THE BRAIN IS AT WORK.

IMMEDIATELY AFTER LYING, A PERSON OFTEN CHANGES ARM OR LEG POSITION.

Reading the Signs

Whether you wish to improve your ability to read the behavior of others in social situations or simply want more control over the messages you are sending, you need to understand the basics of body language. Unconscious physical cues speak volumes, whether during an interview or during an interrogation. So remember:

EYE CONTACT: This most basic element of body language is used to establish trust, to make social connections, or in attempts to seduce. Eye contact lasting more than three seconds usually suggests that confrontation or sex is imminent, while an inability to hold contact indicates that something shifty is afoot.

RAPID EYE BLINK: An extremely revealing sign of emotional stress, possible lying or supreme discomfort. The normal rate is twenty blinks per minute, or one every three seconds, so if you're suspicious about what you're being told, watch for the rapid flutter. If you're the one doing the lying or you don't believe what you're saying, you'd better start staring.

THE CHIN JUT: Often indicative of feelings of superiority, disdain, or skepticism. If you're in some form of confrontation and your opponent is showing lots of neck, you can be sure the resistance is rising. If the actual jaw is being thrust forward, you are in for a real showdown.

ADAM'S APPLE JUMP: More easily spotted in men than in women, the nervous jump indicates embarrassment or emotional anxiety. If it's accompanied by an audible gulp, then serious panic may be setting in. It's one of the more subtle ways you may be sending the "Oh, shit" signal.

BLANK FACE: Generally employed to stonewall or indicate utter lack of interest. It can be used to great effect in public to send a "do not disturb" message, and it's also very useful when one is being investigated by the law.

HEAD TILT: A sign of mild confusion or coy submissiveness, this one requires a bit of interpretation based on the context. In a romantic scenario, it is generally a sign of interest or a signal to proceed. In casual conversation, it may indicate curiosity, but in a business meeting, it usually means you're not making very much sense.

HANDS ON HIPS: An indication of preparedness to take control of a situation. Whether employed in a defensive or offensive fashion, the message is "Oh, I have something to say about this." Excellent for comedians, angry parents, and when one is being dumped.

CROSSED ARMS: Generally taken as a defensive signal of self-protection, this gesture may also indicate skepticism or boredom. Best avoided if you don't want to appear defensive, and important to take note of if you're trying to seduce someone or pitch an idea.

THE BIG EXHALE: Usually an indication of exasperation or disbelief. Also known as a sigh, it can easily be interpreted as a pompous and condescending message, as Al Gore discovered in the 2000 presidential debates. Best used in moderation—save up one big good one for the right moment.

PEEKABOO TONGUE: A brief flash of tongue between the lips can mean one of two things. It is often a sign of impatience or waning interest. Then again, it may signal a preparation to strike. The context of the interaction should tell you whether you're losing them or you're about to be devoured.

THE IMAGINARY FLUFF PICK: Picking lint from the leg or sleeve is a very effective way of saying, "I am losing interest or patience with you," or "I'm going to kill you." A favorite of CEOs and Mafia dons.

THE SUDDEN, WORDLESS DEPARTURE FROM THE ROOM: The closest thing there is to human punctuation. You lose. Period.

Of course, there are countless others, such as the impatient tapping of a foot and the skepticism of the raised eyebrow. But for someone as shrewd and insightful as you, a review of such obvious matters would only result in slightly pursed lips and a disappointed sigh, am I right? You get the idea, so let us move on to something with a bit more flash. Let's get a little mystery going on here.

CHAPTER 7

CREATING MYSTERY

Sex appeal is 50 percent what you've got and 50 percent what people think you've got.

—SOPHIA LOREN

The Ultimate Attraction

From the dawn of time, humankind has always been fascinated by mystery. The great unknown has continuously triggered the imagination and curiosity of human beings and has been the driving force behind all the advances, discoveries, and breakthroughs of societies throughout the ages. The desire and need of the human mind to know the unknowable, and to

understand that which is mystifying, propels us forward magneti-
cally just as surely as gravity holds our feet to the earth. You see
where this is going?

The stars we see in heaven are no different than the stars that walk
among us. We stare at them, wondering, dreaming, and imagining.
What am I really looking at? Is it as it appears to be? Is it very far
away, or is it nearer to me than I realize? Though no one individual
is entirely knowable, those who actually spark our curiosity and
make us wonder about them are the ones we remember. But the gift
is not randomly bestowed upon the lucky. That gift is really no more
than a simple realization.

Whether by intuition or conscious decision, the people who truly
fascinate us have realized at some point that by maintaining some
small part of themselves that is eternally private and largely
unreachable, they generate a magnetism that draws people into
their orbit. It is the reason we fall in love with those who elude us
and dump those who put out immediately and get all clingy. The
reason we dream of wealth is that we wish to know how it feels to be
in that unimaginable state. Sometimes when wealth is realized it is
accompanied by disappointment. The same is true of fame and
landing the objects of our romantic desires. Once they are attained,
the romantic mist of it all seems to evaporate, leaving only reality.

That sense of mystery is what makes people fall in love with the
movie stars they see on-screen. Why? Because we can watch them
intimately, knowing that they cannot see us. We can move in so close
that we feel we could kiss them, because they are seemingly unaware

of our presence. Therein lies the power of brilliant acting, and all great stars know that the closer they allow us to come in, the greater the power they hold over us. It is the power of the closeup, and stars will give you everything in their closeups, because they are protected by the distance of an artificial reality, a soft lens, and flattering lighting. They know that we will project onto them whatever we wish or need to project, and they allow it, sometimes even revel in it. The aura of mystery is created when we allow others to feel that they are very, very close to us, and yet there is something fluttering beyond their reach, distant and intangible.

Magnetism is created when a desire to know and understand more is triggered. It can happen spontaneously with a flash of the eyes that is open to interpretation. Subtle mixed messages, mysterious smiles, and knowing glances pose questions that arouse curiosity. Even small children learn very early that they can attract the attention of adults by fixing their eyes on them and then looking away as soon as eye contact is made. They then return the look and continue the experiment, catching and releasing, testing the limits of their power to control another's attention. Of course, there are other children chasing balls around who don't bother with such things, but those early instincts and games can develop into strong and powerful qualities later in life.

Does this imply that if you liked chasing balls as a child, you have no mystery? Not at all. The primary ingredient of mystery is a simple awareness that in all human interaction, a game is under way. It is not a self-absorbed and manipulative game, nor is it a contest to see who can dominate the other. It is a friendly game of catch and release that can only take off if both parties wish to play. You may knock yourself out trying to lure in an unwilling subject only to come across as a spooky individual with a facial tic if the interest is not there. But with a little practice and experimentation, the senses can be honed, and it becomes very clear who's up for the game and who isn't. One of the secrets of successful flirts is that they are willing to play the game with just about anyone they encounter. However, they also have a keenly developed sense of when to abandon ship, sometimes in order to pique interest, other times to avoid a punch in the nose.

As in any seduction, be it romantic or in a business transaction, you offer up a little and then withdraw. You let out the line and slowly pull it back. Whether you are luring a client toward a deal or luring a lover into the sack, the same rules apply. It's a dance, and it takes time to get the rhythm down.

The Mysterious Balance

When it comes to maintaining your social mystery, balance is essential. You should always keep a certain amount in reserve, but being secretive or aloof will only cause others to lose interest. On the other hand, you never want to bulldoze people with too much information or any hint of desperation:

No one should know how much or how little money you have. An aura of privileged Bohemia is best.

Your sex appeal should be enhanced by flattering and stylish clothing. Trying to buy "sexy" clothes will not give you sex appeal.

Light flirtation and an easy sexuality are very alluring. Sexual desperation and blatant attempts at seduction suggest a big fat sleazeball.

A nice balance between speaking and listening helps you to retain some mystery. Tell them your whole life story and there's nothing left to learn.

Carefully controlled eye contact can generate a lot of intriguing energy. Darting eyes and extended stares can generate a lot of discomfort.

Casual ease in formal situations suggests social sophistication. Sloppy manners and too much familiarity will reveal your shortcomings.

Parceling out information in small doses and hinting at a deeper story keep others interested. Secrecy and dancing around simple questions are just annoying.

Knowing when to leave the party will keep people interested in seeing you again. Stay too long and they'll be interested in getting rid of you for good.

> *There can be no power without mystery. There must always be a "something" which others cannot altogether fathom, which puzzles them, stirs them, and rivets their attention.*
> *—Charles de Gaulle*

Marlene

If ever there was a star who truly understood the importance of mystique, it was Marlene Dietrich. Sadly, the original M has been largely forgotten among the younger generations, but in every sense, the German sex symbol of early cinema embodied the very essence of international allure and scandalous mass appeal.

In her heyday, which was the mid-1930s, Marlene was the original scandalatrix. She wore men's suits, her movies hinted at bisexuality (rent *Morocco*), and she represented a new wave in female sexual assertiveness. American audiences embraced her progressive sexuality because she was foreign and exotic. Had the girl next door engaged in such behavior, she would have been sent packing in a heartbeat. But given the armor of "otherness," she became an object of fascination and a global star to rival Greta Garbo.

Having learned the importance of lighting and angles from the master director Josef von Sternberg, Marlene understood from the very beginning that image was everything. She was impossibly glamorous in each of her roles. Though she surely cared about the quality of the films themselves, Marlene understood that her greatest legacy would come from the still photographs and celluloid images that would eventually elevate her into the pantheon of cinema superstars.

Long after her status as a movie star faded, she embarked on a career of cabaret appearances on a grand scale. She played Las Vegas, London's West End, New York, and any other glamorous capital starved for a true star. The fact that she was a terrible singer was irrelevant. She performed. Completely tone deaf, she acted out her songs with unparalleled theatrical grandiosity. Clad in a white mink over what appeared to be a transparent Jean Louis gown, she croaked her repertoire to enraptured audiences and dazzled the critics through sheer attitude.

But her greatest manipulations were executed after the shows. After each performance, she would slip into her limousine waiting by the backstage door and ride around to the front of the theater. Knowing that the fans would be breathlessly awaiting a glimpse of her, she would have her driver inch the limousine slowly along the curb, barking, "Go slower, slower!" One by one she would slip presigned eight-by-ten photos of herself out the cracked window, relishing the sight of the fans fighting for the souvenirs of a great legend. As the hysteria rose, she would continue feeding photos out the window, slowly, one at a time, orchestrating the mounting chaos. "Slower! Slower!" she would shout. Then, as the limousine reached the corner, she would shout, "NOW FAST!" And with that command, the driver would hit the gas and Marlene would hurl a stack of photos out the window, creating a flurry of desperate scrambling as her limousine sped off around the corner and into the night. Brilliant.

Mystery Boys

It should be pointed out that mystery and magnetism were not the exclusive domain of the film goddesses. Though female stars such as Marilyn Monroe and Brigitte Bardot knew how to project allure and draw fans in, so did many male movie stars. Consider Marlon Brando. He revolutionized American acting by bringing a smoldering sexuality, volatile unpredictability, and troubled vulnerability to the screen that was entirely new at the time. Men related to the complexity of his characters, and women were drawn in by his raw sexual energy, but everyone was transfixed by the sensitivity and emotional turmoil that were simmering just below the surface of this magnetic new screen star. The audiences wanted to figure him out, perhaps even rescue him from himself. (Of course, years later they just wanted to rescue him from his refrigerator.)

In contrast to the early Brando, James Dean and Montgomery Clift were both boyishly handsome and arguably less threatening than

Brando, but they also projected similar forms of cinematic complexity that piqued the curiosity of the audience and made them superstars in their day. The common thread is mystery. And though it's true that boring people sometimes become stars, it is only those who are able to suggest that there is more to them than meets the eye that can truly hold our attention and become legends, even after death.

Of course, much of the hysteria that surrounded stars back then was fully orchestrated by agents, managers, and publicists, who hired hordes of screaming teenage girls for a few dollars each to stand in front of the theaters and go berserk on cue. It was done for Frank Sinatra, Elvis, and the Beatles, and it is a practice still employed today by pop stars and media handlers. After all, if there were no screaming fans to react to, you'd look pretty silly climbing on the roof of an SUV with an umbrella in order to dance outside your trial, wouldn't you?

Of course, such staged shenanigans are entirely unworthy of a naturally magnetic star such as yourself, but that doesn't mean a little hint of turmoil wouldn't add a nice touch to your already-glittering persona. But which mystery is best suited to you?

FIVE OPTIONS TO CRANK UP THE MYSTERY

A TROUBLED BACK STORY: Nothing conjures up feelings of devotion and protectiveness on the part of an audience better than the old wounded-sparrow act. Everyone dreams of finding a forlorn hottie to rescue.

SEXUAL CONFUSION: Troubled messages of "I want to, but I can't," "I'm no good for you," or "There are things you don't know about me" are gold when it comes to eliciting sexual hysteria. Additionally, hints at bisexuality can double your fan base.

LONELINESS: A downturned chin and wide eyes can suggest a deep well of loneliness that will have admirers rushing forward with buckets of love for you. Of this little trick, Princess Diana was a master.

DANGER: Hints of unpredictability and potential drama, whether they're emotional or sexual, can be irresistible and fan the flames of adoration. But try not to go beyond a nicely simmering volatility. There's nothing sexy about a boiling rage.

DEPTH AND WISDOM: Though seemingly less sexy, profound wisdom and a deep intellect can be wildly intoxicating to anyone who dreams of escaping their dull surroundings. Ironically, the appeal is often lost on the stupid, who are either intimidated or too dim to notice.

CANDLES IN THE WIND:

THOUGH HIGHLY INADVISABLE, AN EARLY AND UNTIMELY DEATH OFTEN CEMENTS A LEGEND. BY CHECKING OUT EARLY, THESE STARS BECAME FROZEN IN TIME AND REMAIN FOREVER YOUNG:

JEAN HARLOW—*twenty-six years old*

JAMES DEAN—*twenty-four years old*

BUDDY HOLLY—*twenty-two years old*

MARILYN MONROE—*thirty-six years old*

JANIS JOPLIN—*twenty-seven years old*

JIM MORRISON—*twenty-seven years old*

JIMI HENDRIX—*twenty-seven years old*

KURT COBAIN—*twenty-seven years old*

RIVER PHOENIX—*twenty-three years old*

SELENA—*twenty-three years old*

PRINCESS DIANA—*thirty-six years old*

Entrances and Exits

The art of entering and exiting a social arena is another area worth examining as a great opportunity to create a strong first impression. Though it might appear that such matters only have relevance on the red carpet, the truth is that they are a significant part of our daily lives, and an opportunity that is often wasted by those who are unsavvy in the ways of the stars.

The way that you enter a conference room can create an instant impression of authority or insecurity. Your attitude as you enter a restaurant for a blind date can give you the upper hand or sink you into a position of helplessness. And the very first impression you make in an audition or job interview can seal the deal before your ass ever hits the chair.

The fact is that people tend to think in terms of snapshots when it comes to first impressions. This principle is only heightened at red carpet events, where a sea of flashing bulbs and leering lenses requires that stars be "on" from the moment they stick their leg out of the limo until they are safely hidden behind the door of a bathroom stall. And a true star knows that how you appear as you approach is no more important than how you appear as you depart. After all, everyone is all smiles and flattery when facing you, but it's when you turn to leave that they really zero in and evaluate the dress, the posture, and the posterior. You must look as good from the back as you do from the front.

Granted, a rising starlet needs to pay more attention to the amount of butt cleavage she is willing to reveal than the business executive who has a solid plan to present to the board. But even in the most seemingly benign situations, awareness equals safety. Think of the poor teenage girl who spends hours on her hair, sculpting the bangs and the various shoots and wings that frame her face, yet leaves the back flat as if she just got off a plane after a flight from Australia. Consider the job applicant who ducks into the bathroom for a quick pee, floss, and nostril evaluation. He checks his fly, his tie, and the whiteness of his eyes, but then he strides out with the back of his jacket tucked in his underpants.

Yes, I know it all seems hopelessly small and trivial, but one humiliating episode is all it takes to undermine a lifetime of confidence. So, what do we need to keep in mind? How can we cover our bases? Well, the first thing is to always check the reflection over the shoulder. Beyond that, here's a little checklist to keep in mind for your entrances and exits:

Try not to arrive alone. There is protection in numbers, and you'll look less vulnerable in any situation if you have allies.

If you do arrive alone, don't panic. Just decide where you are going. The seat at the end of the conference table? The bar at the cocktail party? The first person you recognize? Make a decision and execute. The last thing you want is to appear lost.

Survey the room, preferably from an elevated position. Stop at the top of the stairs, or head for an open area from which you can evaluate the scene and choose your target.

Don't be too aloof. Be gracious and open. It's a social situation and others may be in need of a quick friend just as you are. Network.

Keep moving. If you stay in the same place for too long, you become furniture.

Rotate so that people can watch and observe you. Eye contact can be intimidating, and those who are too shy to approach you may think twice after watching you in action.

Start with humor and keep things light. A happy, laughing person is far more intriguing than a morose wallflower.

If someone significant is watching, casually draw attention to your best assets with seemingly random floating hands. Brush your cleavage or check for your wallet.

Make eye contact with as many people as possible, but keep it brief. If there is someone you wish to meet, hold the contact a little longer.

Make a point of mingling and meeting, and charm everyone ruthlessly. You never know.

Don't linger too long. It's like speed dating. After the first round, you'll know who you want to pursue.

The best escape in an awkward situation is to recognize someone across the room, or to excuse yourself and head to the bathroom.

Always have somewhere else you need to be—another meeting, friends waiting, or "all the nominees need to go inside now."

A parting glance over the shoulder as you leave is the best way to signal, "I'll be seeing you again."

I've never been an intellectual but I have this look.
—Woody Allen

The Clever Chameleon

Ever since the early 1980s, when that disgruntled little cheerleader from Detroit thrust herself upon the world stage, we have seen the powerful impact of personal and professional reinvention. Every time we thought we had her pegged, Madonna would emerge with a new persona. And though the concept of a star evolving and changing with the times was nothing new, no one had ever done it with such relentless speed and frequency.

Pop tart, material girl, bisexual superstar, Evita, new-age mystic, grounded mother, rhinestone cowgirl, Englishwoman, and hipster kabbalist are but a few of the presentations she has paraded across our collective consciousness. Some may see it all as pure artifice, while others may read more into it, but it does point out the simple fact that a little reinvention is a good thing from time to time. After all, she's hardly the only one doing a little shape-shifting here and there.

Still, no matter how many times one may seek to reinvent himself or herself, the fact remains that people will always remember you best the way you entered the party. And so, despite a truly remarkable and prolific career, you can bet that in the distant future, when Madonna is being eulogized, a clip will be playing in the background of her writhing around on the floor in a white wedding dress.

AS FOR YOUR OWN GLORIOUS SELF, TAKE A LESSON FROM MADGE. OR IS IT ESTHER NOW? WHATEVER. HERE ARE SOME EASY WAYS TO REFRESH THAT TIRED OLD IMAGE OF YOURS:

CHANGE YOUR HAIR

CHANGE YOUR WARDROBE

CHANGE YOUR STYLE

CHANGE YOUR BODY

CHANGE YOUR LOVERS

CHANGE YOUR HUSBAND

CHANGE YOUR FRIENDS

CHANGE YOUR OUTLOOK

CHANGE YOUR AGENT

CHANGE YOUR PRODUCER

CHANGE YOUR COUNTRY OF RESIDENCE

CHANGE YOUR ACCENT

CHANGE YOUR RELIGION

CHANGE YOUR NAME

JUST KEEP CHANGING, DAMMIT!

David Hasselhoff and the Big Lie

Speaking of international "superstars," David Hasselhoff and his people have been lying to us. Now, it is not uncommon for major stars to develop large followings abroad. Apparently Jerry Lewis is considered a genius in France. Tom Cruise is big in Japan. And Brad Pitt may be a huge star in the United States, but he is even more popular abroad. That makes him supremely "bankable" even if his movies only do so-so box office in the States. And many U.S. pop bands pay their dues and build followings in foreign markets before they are presented to the U.S. public: "Oh, yes. They sold out stadiums in Bulgaria!"

Stories of successes elsewhere create intrigue: "Perhaps I should rethink my opinion of this person." Which brings us back to David Hasselhoff. For years we have heard that he is a huge singing sensation in Germany. Well, I was recently in Germany and decided to investigate this most curious phenomenon. In every instance, the mere mention of the name drew peels of laughter and hearty knee slaps: "Ach! He ist heeedious!" According to those with whom I spoke, Mr. Hasselhoff is more an icon of American kitsch than the revered singing superstar he would have us believe. Oh, I'm sure he sold some records and has some fans, but it appears that there has been a touch of embellishment somewhere along the way. But why judge? There is a lesson to be learned here.

It can be highly effective to tell someone who is on the fence about you, "Oh, yes. My book of poems just *flew* off the shelves in eastern Europe." Of course, it's best if your claim is true, but even if it's not, it never hurts to create the impression that you are deeply appreciated elsewhere, whether it's in a foreign country, in the minds and esteem of your ex-lovers, or at the last company you worked for. Just slip them a little food for thought and let them wonder why.

Disturbing the Air

Now, let us shift gears and return to the serious business of creating genuine mystique, which is the aura of mystery or mystical powers. Most people find themselves attracted to very subtle undercurrents of sexual danger, edgy humor, or untapped power. The sense that anything could happen at any moment can be very intoxicating. It can be seen in the steely calm of a business executive in a tense negotiation. It can be felt when charismatic actors step onto the stage, even before they speak. And it can be sensed in the secure pauses of a powerful speaker who is commanding her audience.

By teasing your audience—of one or of millions—with hints of unpredictability, you can project a very subtle edge that will draw people toward you. You don't actually need to do anything unpredictable—just lobbing out the hint is usually sufficient. However, if you try too hard, you may end up pushing people away. The key, as always, is subtlety. The moment your efforts become visible, the effect is diminished and you run the risk of looking deliberate or even foolish. By simply focusing on your intention, and trusting that the effect will come if you can resist pushing, you can generate a great deal of energy that can be very

My advice to those who think they have to take off their clothes to be a star is, once you're boned, what's left to create the illusion? Let 'em wonder. I never believed in giving them too much of me.
—Mae West

mesmerizing. In order to ensure subtlety, think of the goal as being no more than creating a very slight disturbance in the air.

DO NOT BE AFRAID OF SILENCE: Silence can command attention. You do not need to speak the moment you enter a room or take to the stage. Take possession of the silence.

ZERO IN ON INDIVIDUALS: Speaking directly to people, and even into them, has far greater impact than directing your words into the open air.

NEVER BECOME DEFENSIVE: Even when directly confronted, a calm and confident response is the most powerful one. Lose your cool and you're at an instant disadvantage.

EXAMINE WHAT IS PRESENTED TO YOU: Whether it's an idea, an offer, a person, or a setting, take time to evaluate the subject at hand. Never allow your decision to be rushed.

SMILE WHEN YOU ARE INSULTED: It will give you time to think through your response, if you choose to respond at all. Sometimes a calm, silent smile is enough to make them regret their words.

Modified Monikers

We all know that Marilyn Monroe was born Norma Jean Baker, and that Cary Grant was really Archibald Leach. It was standard practice in the golden age of Hollywood to completely reinvent an actor's persona by creating a new identity, but many of us reinvent ourselves in smaller ways by subtly changing names as we move through life. Doesn't little Billy usually shift over to William at some point? Or maybe it's just Bill or Will. Each one conjures up different images, and so we choose how we wish to be addressed in order to create an impression.

In many cases, our names precede us, and they can be a curse or a blessing. A girl named Muffin will surely find it a struggle to be taken seriously in her political career. So, how about you? Is your name spectacularly unique, or hopelessly drab? If you're considering a change of your own, you can begin by trying these standard methods of finding an alternative name:

> **YOUR HOLLYWOOD NAME:** This consists of your middle name followed by the name of the street you grew up on.

> **YOUR PORNO NAME:** Take the name of your very first pet, and follow that with the model of your very first car.

How did those work out? Not so great? If you feel less than inspired by your Hollywood and/or porno names, consider the following variations or flat-out deceptions adopted by these well-known celebs who are not who they claim to be. Perhaps inspiration will strike.

> **TORI AMOS**—*Myra Ellen Amos*

> **ADAM ANT**—*Stuart Leslie Goddard*

> **BONO**—*Paul David Hewson*

> **DAVID BOWIE**—*David Robert Hayward-Jones*

> **JACKIE CHAN**—*Fong See Long*

CHEVY CHASE—*Cornelius Crane Chase*

COOLIO—*Artis Ivey, Jr.*

ALICE COOPER—*Vincent Damon Furnier*

DAVID COPPERFIELD—*David Kotkin*

ELVIS COSTELLO—*Declan Patrick McManus*

PORTIA DE ROSSI—*Mandy Rogers*

VIN DIESEL—*Mark Vincent*

WHOOPI GOLDBERG—*Caryn Johnson*

MACY GRAY—*Natalie McIntyre*

BILLY IDOL—*William Board*

ELTON JOHN—*Reginald Kenneth Dwight*

SPIKE JONZE—*Adam Spiegel*

ALICIA KEYS—*Alicia Augello Cook*

BARRY MANILOW—*Barry Alan Pincus*

MARILYN MANSON—*Brian Warner*

RICKY MARTIN—*Enrique Martin Morales*

TIM MCGRAW—*Samuel Timothy Smith*

MEAT LOAF —*Marvin Lee Aday*

GEORGE MICHAEL —*Georgios Panayiotou*

MOBY —*Richard Melville Hall*

DEMI MOORE —*Demetria Gene Guynes*

IGGY POP —*James Jewell Osterberg, Jr.*

JOAN RIVERS —*Joan Sandra Molinsky*

WINONA RYDER —*Winona Horowitz*

GENE SIMMONS —*Chaim Witz*

ANNA NICOLE SMITH —*Vickie Lynn Hogan*

STING —*Gordon Matthew Sumner*

REESE WITHERSPOON —*Laura Jean Reese Witherspoon*

***AND** (I can't help myself, I just keep finding more and more!)*
SOME CLASSIC OLDIES:

WOODY ALLEN —*Allen Stewart Konigsberg*

BRIGITTE BARDOT —*Camille Javal*

ROBERT BLAKE —*Michael Gubitosi*

MICHAEL CAINE —*Maurice J. Micklewhite*

JOAN CRAWFORD—*Lucille Fay LeSueur*

RODNEY DANGERFIELD—*Jacob Cohen*

JOHN DENVER—*Henry John Deutschendorf*

BO DEREK—*Mary Cathleen Collins*

MORGAN FAIRCHILD—*Patsy Ann McClenny*

AUDREY HEPBURN—*Edda van Heemstra Hepburn-Ruston*

BILLIE HOLIDAY—*Eleanora Fagan*

LARRY KING—*Larry Zieger*

JERRY LEWIS—*Joseph Levitch*

SOPHIA LOREN—*Sofia Villani Scicolone*

STEFANIE POWERS—*Stefdnia Zofija Federkiewicz*

SIGOURNEY WEAVER—*Susan Weaver*

RAQUEL WELCH—*Raquel Tejada*

STEVIE WONDER—*Steveland Judkins*

Finally, after all this talk of calculated name changes, I must pay homage to the very best drag name I ever heard. Wherever she is, God bless Lois Commondenominator.

Star Signs

When considering the realms of the mysterious, an examination of zodiacal destiny shows us once again that the stars always play a part in the fate of the stars. And while fame does not discriminate between the signs, the way in which you rise to the top, the reasons behind your drive, and the likely results can be guessed at fairly accurately.

CAPRICORN: Your ambition, willpower, and appreciation of humor will work to your advantage, though your pessimism and consistent crankiness will aggravate your assistants to no end. If you do become a star you will be a nightmare.

Star goats: *Howard Hughes, Faye Dunaway, Joseph Stalin*

AQUARIUS: Friendliness, honesty, and originality are all well and good, but it's your disdain for reality, your unpredictability, and your tendency to lie that will really work in your favor. You will make a puzzling celebrity and be a subject of much gossip.

Star water carriers: *John Travolta, Farrah Fawcett, Dan Quayle*

PISCES: Your intuition, idealism, and imagination will set up some nifty dreams for you to pursue, but your sensitivity and secretive nature may end up causing a few meltdowns when you finally reach the top. Lots of shrink bills and a trip to rehab and/or prison would not surprise.

Star fish: *Tammy Faye Bakker, Johnny Cash, Liza Minelli*

ARIES: Enthusiasm, confidence, and courage will spring from your ridiculously stubborn nature. Your quick wit will be great in interviews, but your selfishness, quick temper, and impatience will make you a very high-maintenance star indeed.

Star rams: *Aretha Franklin, Marlon Brando, Vincent Van Gogh*

TAURUS: Your patience, warm heart, and love of security will need to be conquered ASAP. Luckily, your darker traits of jealousy, greed, and psychotic determination should ensure a strong commitment to success as you scratch and claw your way to the top.

Star bulls: *Sigmund Freud, Eva Perón, Cher*

GEMINI: Versatility, a sense of humor, and good instincts are excellent qualities for a star on the rise. Of course, your nervous tension, superficiality, and schizoid nature will fuel lots of drama and make you a favorite of the tabloids.

Star twins: *Angelina Jolie, Nicole Kidman, Boy George*

CANCER: Your innate sense of caution, high level of sensitivity, and penchant to bury your head in the sand must be overcome. However, your touchiness and general moodiness will make you a vengeful and high-strung celebrity worth watching.

Star crabs: *Princess Diana, Ernest Hemingway, George W. Bush*

LEO: The greatest of all spotlight hogs. Your vanity, ruthless ambition, and lust for attention make you a prime candidate for major stardom. Hopefully, your creativity and charm will help conceal your diabolical plans for world domination. Most Leos would murder to be famous.

Star cats: *Madonna, Whitney Houston, Bill Clinton*

VIRGO: Your modesty, meticulousness, and practicality must be transcended if your star is to shine brightly. On the flip side, your calculated control and critical perfectionism will fuel your ambition and make you a big star who's a major pain in the ass.

Star virgins: *Greta Garbo, Peter Sellers, Sophia Loren*

LIBRA: Your diplomatic, sociable, and modest nature will enable you to schmooze up a storm and rise to the top. However, your unusually strong sex drive and unbridled greed will create an addiction to fame for which there is no cure.

Star scales: *Suzanne Somers, Sting, Martina Navratilova*

SCORPIO: Extreme passion, power, and magnetism will propel you toward the light with great force. You know what you want and you're not afraid to use that nasty little stinger of yours to get it. Scorpios are the most likely of the signs to sleep their way to the top.

Star stingers: *Marie Antoinette, Pablo Picasso, Prince Charles*

SAGITTARIUS: Happy-go-lucky, enthusiastic, and optimistic, Sagittarians make colorful celebrities who often reap the benefits of dumb luck. However, bouts of depression, irresponsibility, and pharmaceutical problems will ensure lots of fun peaks and valleys for the biography.

Star archers: *Jimi Hendrix, Bruce Lee, Bette Midler*

From this highly scientific analysis, we can see that regardless of one's astrological sign, there are potential perils and pitfalls for all. Now, how the slippery skid toward stardom is managed is up to the individual, but it would appear that none are immune to the possibility of a scandalous episode or two along the way. But scandal is not necessarily a bad thing. In fact, it might be just what the doctor ordered.

CHAPTER 8

THE IMPORTANCE OF

SCANDAL

I used to be Snow White . . . but I drifted.

—MAE WEST

What Did You Do?

Remember that oddly homoerotic photo shoot you agreed to just after you graduated college? That seemingly innocent tryst with an underling who kept a journal at your last job? That hilarious videotape of you and your friends partying naked in Palm Springs? Remember your sense of liberating exhilaration as you threw caution to the wind? Well, my friend, it was all documented, and it's all still out there.

In the age of twenty-four-hour surveillance, blogomania, and media empires built on scandal, the excesses of youth and the flights of fancy that make life worth living no longer tend to disappear into the past once the adventure has been lived. Au contraire. Somebody, somewhere, is holding the evidence. And the higher you rise, the more profitable your past peccadilloes become. Does this mean that you must abandon your dreams of superstardom? Is there something out there that will prove to be your Achilles' heel, your ultimate unraveling? Not if you play your cards right. In fact, that old scandal may come in very handy one day.

Anyone who has had a life of any interest whatsoever has dabbled in something scandalous. And those things that in the past may have sunk careers now often make careers. As long as your youthful (or middle-aged) "lapses in judgment" don't involve murder or terrorism, chances are you can survive them. But like a Boy Scout in the woods, you must be prepared.

"I needed the money"; "I had a drinking problem at the time"; "We were in love and I never thought it would be released on DVD"— all perfectly valid deflections these days. Given the rate of professional recovery of disgraced politicians, humiliated movie stars, and imprisoned media moguls, you shouldn't worry too much about your own little indiscretions. In the grand scheme of things, the world at large has become very forgiving, so don't beat yourself up. Just think of a clever quip.

When nude photos of Marilyn Monroe scandalized the nation in the 1950s, a reporter stupidly asked her, "Didn't you have anything on?" Her response was "Oh, yes. I had the radio on." You see? Nothing deflects the disapproving stink-eye of the public so quickly as a witty retort. Of course, humor works better in the face of a little nudity than it does in response to embezzlement, but the point is that a quick wit can sometimes get you out of a sticky wicket. So, should we go out of our way to invite scandal? No. You can do very well with a clean record in this world, but you can't cave in if the world finds out you're a little more colorful than they thought. Sure, people love to gossip and pass judgment, but a wise star on the rise knows that a little spice adds to any recipe.

Everyone has a complicated story, and if you want to get ahead in life, you cannot wither when your past is called into question. When we are young, we all fear judgment and we believe that we will be scrutinized and labeled. But the fact is that no one can judge us as harshly as we judge ourselves. The assumption that everyone is watching our every move comes from a misguided belief that everyone cares. You may be the center of your own universe, but you must understand that everyone else is viewing the world from their own orbital center. And if that's the case, no matter how famous you become, your escapades may be noted, but they can never compete with the obsession people have with their own lives.

Judgment is a fleeting thing, and the public has a very short attention span. It's like kindergarten, really. You just have to wait for the next kid to pee his pants. Thoughts pass, words are printed, and in the end, you have only yourself to answer to. So, own your scandals, and if you forgive yourself, chances are everyone else will move on.

Cultivating Interest

Once you accept that the whole world is not breathlessly awaiting your next move, you'll begin to understand that you can actually benefit from a little hint of scandal here and there. This is not to suggest that you should willingly engage in stupid, self-destructive behavior, but that a little mystery goes a very long way.

One of the keys to cultivating an air of mystery and danger is to keep people guessing. Though people may be less judgmental and unforgiving than you initially imagined, they can still be gossipy and easily scandalized. So why not throw a few bread crumbs to the pigeons? Questions provoke interest. Just keep the ball in play and keep the questions alive.

A person of solid character will always tell the truth, but a little ambiguity is a very alluring thing. And by keeping the questions open, you are not only retaining interest, you are also keeping your own options open. You know what you feel and what you believe, but you don't need to reveal your entire psyche every time someone asks a simple question. It's not secrecy, and it's not deception. It's only caution, because after all, we all have our moments of indiscretion.

SO, YOU'RE STILL FEELING A BIT QUEASY ABOUT YOUR SCANDALOUS SELF? DON'T SWEAT IT, BABE. YOU'RE NOT THE FIRST ONE TO FALL OFF THE PEDESTAL. GIVE YOURSELF A BREAK:

FORGIVE YOURSELF FOR EVERYTHING SHORT OF MURDER, PEDOPHILIA, AND CRUELTY TO ANIMALS.

ACCEPT YOUR SEXUAL SELF AND ANY AMBIGUITY
THAT COMES WITH IT.

LEARN FROM YOUR MISTAKES.

RETHINK YOUR JUDGMENT OF OTHERS.

EMBRACE THE ATTRACTIVENESS OF MILD SCANDAL.

ENJOY YOUR OWN MYSTERY.

ALLOW YOURSELF TO EXPERIMENT WITHIN REASON.

GET OVER YOURSELF.

Learning from the Masters: Top Celebrity Scandals

BILL CLINTON AND MONICA LEWINSKY

MINOR INFRACTION: Bill and Monica engage in a few run-of-the-mill debriefings.

HYSTERIA LEVEL: Off the charts.

TITILLATION FACTOR: Enough to bring hundreds of Republicans to the brink of orgasm.

RECOVERY: Slick Willie pulls through, but Monica flees D.C. to sell handbags.

He looked good under arrest. I loved the handcuffs—they always work. Criminal movie star is a really good look for Johnny.
—John Waters on Johnny Depp's arrest for trashing a hotel room

PARIS HILTON SEX TAPE

There are two types of people in this world, good and bad. The good sleep better, the bad seem to enjoy the waking hours much more.
–Woody Allen

MINOR INFRACTION: Scientifically minded heiress conducts experiment with night-vision camcorder.

HYSTERIA LEVEL: Inexplicably high.

TITILLATION FACTOR: Millions cackle with glee at the hapless Hilton.

RECOVERY: Complete. Obviously, that was only the opening act in an ongoing production.

JANET JACKSON'S SUPERBOOB

MINOR INFRACTION: Janet chooses to show off some new jewelry.

HYSTERIA LEVEL: Conservatives go ape shit; the rest of us have seen one before.

TITILLATION FACTOR: Too easy.

RECOVERY: Thanks to Michael, she's still considered the sane Jackson.

MARTHA STEWART GOES TO JAIL

MINOR INFRACTION: Martha tells a crisp little fib to make a pesky situation go away.

HYSTERIA LEVEL: A media frenzy ensues, and Martha is transformed into Marie Antoinette.

TITILLATION FACTOR: Not very sexy, but delicious to all who have suffered her inhospitality.

RECOVERY: Fully stage-managed and highly profitable. Martha is now a sweetie.

LEONA HELMSLEY GOES TO JAIL

MINOR INFRACTION: Uttering "Only the little people pay taxes" in front of the little people.

HYSTERIA LEVEL: Significant in its day, but moderate in hindsight.

TITILLATION FACTOR: Fun to see the "Queen of Mean" wondering aloud how people can be so cruel.

RECOVERY: Who knows? Is she out yet?

GEORGE MICHAEL BATHROOM INCIDENT

MINOR INFRACTION: Submitting to an officer of the law.

HYSTERIA LEVEL: Relatively moderate due to declining star status.

TITILLATION FACTOR: Very titillating, apparently.

RECOVERY: Irrelevant. He's retired from the spotlight anyway.

JIM AND TAMMY FAYE BAKKER SCANDAL

MINOR INFRACTION: Embezzling a few million from lonely old ladies.

HYSTERIA LEVEL: Adequately high given the ungodly greed.

TITILLATION FACTOR: Increased by revelations of air-conditioned dog houses and improper sexual conduct.

Life is a great big canvas; throw all the paint on it you can.
—Danny Kaye

RECOVERY: Never achieved. You can mess around, but you can't mess with God.

JIMMY SWAGGART: "I HAVE SINNED!"

MINOR INFRACTION: Trying to save a hooker through cocaine therapy.

HYSTERIA LEVEL: Pretty high, as was Jimmy.

TITILLATION FACTOR: Hypocrisy always makes for good fun.

RECOVERY: Unknown. Has anyone seen him lately? Is he still alive?

HUGH GRANT: KNOBGATE

MINOR INFRACTION: Uptight Brit seeks Divine release.

HYSTERIA LEVEL: Worthy of a *Tonight Show* confession.

TITILLATION FACTOR: Cheap sex heightened by Liz Hurley's silent rage. Fun stuff.

RECOVERY: Foppish British charm trumps all. No harm done.

ZSA ZSA SLAPS A COP

MINOR INFRACTION: Aging actress experiments with S&M.

HYSTERIA LEVEL: Fairly low due to the advanced age of the accused.

TITILLATION FACTOR: Negligible. No saucy visions of *Caged Heat* here.

RECOVERY: Sure, whatever, it was funny.

WINONA RYDER'S STICKY FINGERS

MINOR INFRACTION: Shopping on painkillers.

HYSTERIA LEVEL: Enough to sell "Free Winona" T-shirts.

TITILLATION FACTOR: Zero, given the demure courtroom wardrobe.

RECOVERY: Subject emerges seemingly unscathed.

ROBERT DOWNEY, JR., TAKES A NAP

MINOR INFRACTION: Napping in a neighbor's home during a chemical bender.

HYSTERIA LEVEL: Moderate. No one was in the bed with him.

TITILLATION FACTOR: Again, no one was in the bed with him.

RECOVERY: Complete. Now a mere footnote in the rehab annals.

TONYA HARDING HAS NANCY KERRIGAN CLUBBED

MINOR INFRACTION: Ice witch hires hit man to improve Olympic chances.

HYSTERIA LEVEL: Global media field day.

TITILLATION FACTOR: Catfight on ice equals highest Olympic ratings ever.

RECOVERY: No. It's all mug shots and misdemeanors now.

COURTNEY LOVE INSISTS ON BEING COURTNEY LOVE

MINOR INFRACTION: Yes, several, and also major infractions.

HYSTERIA LEVEL: Amazingly sustained by perpetual episodes.

TITILLATION FACTOR: Largely based on how disheveled she appears in court.

RECOVERY: Undetermined.

FARRAH LOSES FOCUS ON LETTERMAN

MINOR INFRACTION: Appearing on television high as a kite.

HYSTERIA LEVEL: Maxes out at the level of infotainment television.

TITILLATION FACTOR: Messy fun and good water-cooler fodder.

RECOVERY: Sure, what the hell. She's still watchable.

So, what conclusions can we draw from these stellar examples of scandal? Recovery seems to be fairly common, so perhaps a carefully crafted shocker might not be such a bad thing after all. But which types of scandal result in the most ink? Since you're already armed with a deep understanding of the importance of self-forgiveness, you might as well go for the gold. In order:

SEXCAPADES: Always most effective if a home is wrecked or a career is ruined. In order for the scandal to really have legs, though, make sure your antics are photographed or videotaped.

PUBLIC MELTDOWN: Chalk it up to exhaustion if you must, but increasingly erratic behavior fueled by alcohol, drugs, and emotional fragility makes for great television and lots of publicity.

ASSAULT: An old standby, the sneak attack on a member of the paparazzi guarantees coverage in the tabloids. But for maximum interest, nothing comes close to a catfight in a nightclub.

PUBLIC NUDITY: Falling down on the red carpet with no underwear trumps all, but a seemingly accidental flash or a naked stretch on a hotel balcony captured by the press will ensure tabloid coverage.

FINANCIAL TRICKERY: Not the sexiest of options, and the result is often a humiliating celebrity perp walk and jail time. Still, if the sentence is a short one, you may get to start over as the underdog, with a book deal.

SHOPLIFTING: As cries for attention go, this is definitely the least glamorous of all. The overhead angles of department-store video cameras are rarely flattering, and it's humiliating to be busted by a security guard.

Damage Control

Once the deed has been done, or more specifically, once the deed has been discovered, you can be sure the media will be giddy with delight at the prospect of covering your every move. Therefore, it behooves the guilty (or in your case, the falsely accused!) to remember a few standard star tricks for your courthouse appearances:

Always arrive in sunglasses. No need to let the press see that you were up all night drinking and crying.

Get your parents to show up. The older and more frightened they look, the better.

Dress modestly so that the public may see how surprisingly conservative you are offstage.

Keep quiet and look as sad and pathetic as possible as your lawyer addresses the media.

If things are looking grim, show up with a broken limb or a neck brace.

If your defense is completely falling apart, faint on the witness stand.

If you're convicted, don't sweat it. A short stay at a minimum-security prison is the new rehab. You can sober up, lose some weight, and reemerge as a transformed angel.

Watch Your Step

Would you be offended if I said I was a bit worried about you? I mean, you really perked up during the scandalous stuff—much more than during the previous chapters. You're not going to get carried away are you? I mean, we have to be careful in regard to that tawdry streak of yours. You know how you can be.

All right, I'll say no more. You've come this far and I can only assume you know what you're doing. I shall simply let the bird fly. I have done my best to convince you that this is a tricky game, and I have warned you of the dangers. But clearly you are eager to leave our comfy little nest, and I will not be accused of holding you back. Let us move on. That is, if you don't mind my tagging along to watch.

CHAPTER 9

NOW THAT YOU'RE A STAR

There is less in this than meets the eye.

—TALLULAH BANKHEAD

Watch Your Back

Let me just say this. Now that you are a star, you can bet there will be slings and arrows hurtling in your direction with alarming regularity. The simple fact is that success breeds skepticism, and as soon as you reach a certain level of notoriety and recognition, others will begin to wonder, why you and not them? People will begin to project their own bitterness and

Fame is a vapor; popularity an accident; the only earthly certainty is oblivion.
–Mark Twain

envy onto you. They will say what they think of you, sometimes in hushed whispers and sometimes to your face. But chances are that if you have the psychotic drive and confidence required to become a star in the first place, you've probably already got a fairly thick skin, so the screeching howler monkeys and squawking parrots shouldn't really ruffle your feathers too much.

Even so, awareness is preparation, and it pays to be prepared as you move through the treacherous jungle of celebrity. You'll need a guide, an ally, a confidant, and a few dispensable underlings you can throw to the lions when things get a bit hairy. Let's not be coy at this late stage of the game. The path to success is always littered with the carcasses of those who had to be sacrificed along the way. If they're not quick enough, they get left behind. If they're not helping you anymore, then you don't need them anymore. And woe to those who try and stand in your way.

Am I right? Do you understand now how the game works? Are you feeling the power? If so, you have fallen right into the very first pothole of success. If the first little flash of success is going to send you into an egomaniacal frenzy, you'll be cutting ribbons at supermarket openings before the first check clears. Yes, you need to watch out for yourself, and yes, you are in a precarious position, but don't get swept away just yet. You may not yet be quite as famous as you think. (Suckah!)

The Levels of Fame

Fame, like obesity, must be measured in degrees. While some may simply be bloated with delusions of their own grandeur, there are others who are genuinely plump with recognition. Beyond that, there are those who achieve significant girth in terms of publicity and "ink," and those who become notably fat with fame. (Or as they say on the street, *phat*.) And finally, at the far end of the scale, there are the morbidly famous who find it extremely difficult just to move about.

However, no one reaches the morbid levels of fame overnight. We all start out with roughly the same magnetic metabolism, but it is only those who continue to feed the monster that come to reach gargantuan proportions. Fame is never an accident. Notoriety or infamy may occur unexpectedly through scandal or crime, but true sustained fame can only be achieved through tremendous greed and a truly insatiable appetite for attention.

Only a steady and consistent diet of shameless self-promotion, regular forays into the spotlight, and opportunities recognized and seized can expand one's star status to the screen-filling extreme. And this formula does not apply exclusively to movie stars and pop icons. It is very much in evidence wherever and whenever mere mortals set out to join the ranks of the earthbound stars. Recognition is not so much based on merit these days as it is the result of strategically tooting one's own horn. After all, you can't expect to shine if you're hiding in the shadows.

Of course, there are those who will say that humility and modesty prevent them from engaging in something so unseemly as self-promotion, but these dismal characters underestimate the subtlety that can be applied to such endeavors. By focusing on the desired results, you can find perfectly acceptable ways of drawing attention to your achievements or simply highlighting your star potential. On the other hand, you never want to draw attention to your shortcomings, so when in public, keep the following in mind:

DO play up to the photographers.

DON'T start flipping them off until you're financially secure.

DO make a point of charming every interviewer.

DON'T be difficult or surly unless you're cultivating a nasty rebel reputation.

DO make an effort to look your best at public functions.

DON'T end up in the tabloids fueling rumors of a meltdown.

DO master the art of the sound bite.

DON'T ramble on in interviews boring everyone with your true thoughts.

DO make a practice of speaking well of other famous people.

DON'T trash your fellow celebs unless you need the publicity of a star war.

DO be gracious to your new gushing fans.

DON'T bust their bubble by revealing how unworthy you are.

So, there you have the basics of Fame 101, but if you really want to make the leap to the next level, you'll need to delegate the management of your public persona. In many cases, a parent or spouse will naturally step into the role of your personal cheerleader and adviser. It might be a professional mentor, or it could be as simple as joining forces with a close friend who will agree to promote you and your cause as you agree to promote theirs. But to really make the leap into the big leagues, you'll probably need to spend a little cash. Enter the publicist.

Who Is Tara Reid?

Honestly, I have no idea. I have never seen her in any movie or television program, but from what I gather she is an actress. As of the writing of these words, I have never even heard her speak, yet somehow, I am aware of her presence on the planet and the state of her left breast. In fact, I recently saw in the *TV Guide* that she has actually warranted an episode of *Biography* all her own. By no means do I intend to besmirch her name or potential talent—for all I know she may be an amazing actress or she may be totally talent-free. Again, I am clueless. But the mere fact that I can recognize her in photographs and put a face to the name is a testament to the power of publicity.

Clearly, someone has been paid a significant sum of cash to make sure that I know who she is. There is a publicist at work here, and apparently a very good one at that. Because of this publicist's efforts, I am aware that Ms. Reid is a party girl on the rise, that she is a player in young Hollywood, and that I would be lucky to have such a promising starlet in my next film, should I ever choose to produce one. If everyone else knows about her, then there must be some "there" there, and no price could be too exorbitant should she bless my production with her fabulous star power.

Celebrity in the twenty-first century is such that name recognition precedes talent. Granted, there are many celebrities who have earned their place in the public consciousness through years of hard work, achievement, and accomplishment. However, there is also a new breed of celebrity in the mix whose value is measured in terms of recognizability.

At this point in time, there is no one on earth who exemplifies this phenomenon more clearly than the ubiquitous Paris Hilton. She is famous for nothing. She is simply famous because she is famous. To be fair, I may have missed some heart-wrenching performance of hers in some gritty independent film, or a particularly touching episode of her "reality" program, but something deep inside me tells me that I have missed nothing. And while her platinum hair extensions and micromini ensembles make her reasonably photogenic, she is not so gloriously beautiful that she eclipses all those that surround her. No. Ms. Hilton is the employer of a frantically busy publicist who tells her where to be seen and how to attract attention, plots her "career" moves, arranges her various appearances, and spins her weekly disasters. The fact is that despite all outward appearances, the press is not chasing Paris Hilton; she is chasing them.

In this day and age, anyone who is even remotely recognizable knows better than to have sex in front of a video camera. And the shock and coyly exhibited hurt expressed by Hilton when the tapes became public were a laughably transparent bid for attention and sympathy: "Oh, the poor thing, her innocence and naïveté exploited by some cad." That little meeting with the publicist must have been a summit of high comedy. But the funny behind the funny was that the harebrained scheme worked like a charm. She was in the news! She was being downloaded! Her tearful parents were interviewed as her stock was rising. Her profile was on the upswing as her dignity sank, and really, that is all a simple working girl could hope for. Once the fever pitch of media coverage reached its height, all that was needed was to insert a career. I'm sure they'll think of something.

The true merit of a good publicist is the ability to make it all seem spontaneous. As the public scratches its collective head, murmuring phrases like "I don't see why she's such a big deal," the simple truth is that she's not. Aside from a handful of megastars, any celebrity is perfectly capable of dropping off the radar at a moment's notice. There is always fresh, young meat just dying to step into the spotlight once a vacancy opens up, and in order to remain in the public eye, a "star" must continue to feed the machine and pay the publicist.

So how does this notion apply to the average person hoping to raise his or her profile? By now you should know. You must learn to toot your own horn. And now that you are in the spotlight, you'll need to hang on to that light. How?

GIVE INTERVIEWS.

GET YOURSELF PHOTOGRAPHED.

LAUNCH A WEB SITE.

KEEP TRACK OF YOUR CONTACTS.

NETWORK.

SCHMOOZE.

Hollywood is lone-
liness beside the
swimming pool.
—Liv Ullmann

ACCEPT INVITATIONS.

CHANGE YOUR PHONE NUMBER.

GET A STYLIST.

CREATE A SCANDAL.

DATE A CELEBRITY.

DUMP THAT CELEBRITY BEFORE BEING DUMPED.

PRETEND TO BE INTERESTED IN CHARITIES.

HOST *SATURDAY NIGHT LIVE.*

ADOPT A CAUSE.

Don't kid yourself. It's like having children. Your life is no longer your own.

Vocabulary of the Stars

Once a certain level of fame has been achieved, life itself begins to change. Not on the deeper levels, perhaps, but on the surface one begins to realize that fame not only affects our own behavior, but that of those around us as well. New challenges and considerations arise as new situations present themselves.

By the time you've become intimately familiarized with the invasive paparazzi, the endless PR requests, the unnerving suggestions of plastic surgery, and the intricate rules of the fame game, you'll probably realize that your old vocabulary is insufficient to describe your surreal new world. As with all types of travel, it helps to know the lingo once you're not in Kansas anymore:

ANONYMOUSE: An individual at a public function who lurks in the shadows and is entirely devoid of charisma or electricity.

BOTOXICATION: The appearance of emotional numbness or pharmaceutical inebriation brought on by excessive use of Botox.

BRUISE CRUISE: A brief period of absenteeism from the spotlight while you're recovering from plastic surgery.

BUNGEE HUMPING: The practice of swiftly rushing into a new high-profile romance immediately after being publicly dumped.

CELEBARAZZI: B-list celebrities who desperately rush toward photographers rather than the other way around (Trash!).

CELEBAURANT: An eatery the notoriety of which is entirely based on the fame of its investors.

DREAMCICLE: A delusional or unrealistic aspiration or expectation that will eventually melt away and/or fall off.

FAGNETISM: An inherent quality of a star that makes him or her wildly appealing to the gay community.

FAME FLOP: An intentional, though seemingly accidental, popping out of a bodily appendage on camera—usually executed in a desperate bid for attention.

FLASH HOLE: A particularly aggressive, obnoxious, or invasive photographer.

GLOBAL CORRIDOR: The unfortunate and unnatural chasm formed between the boobs as a result of an overly ambitious breast augmentation.

GOOGLICIOUS: A level of celebrity achieved when a simple Internet search produces copious quantities of nude photos and salacious gossip about an individual.

HOMOSWITCHUALITY: A publicly declared reversal of sexual orientation—in either direction—intended to raise one's public profile and draw publicity.

HOOKERELLA: An individual who achieves a brief flash of fame and attention resulting from a tawdry sexcapade.

IN-FLIGHT WHOOPSIE BAG: An aging sex symbol who appears at a public function clearly hopped up on pills.

JUNKET SPUNK: False enthusiasm generated by celebrities when forced to publicize a really bad movie or lack-luster product. (Well, that's one definition, anyway.)

LACKTOR/LACKTRESS: A screen thespian of questionable talent.

MODELIMIA: A disorder characterized by the firm belief that human life can be sustained on an exclusive diet of cigarettes, lettuce, and champagne.

TELEPOLOGY: A touching and heartfelt taped or live address to a global audience intended to convey innocence or regret after the shit hits the fan.

TROUT MOUTH: A gruesome fishlike appearance brought on by excessive pumping of collagen into the lips.

Longevity

You know what they say. As hard as it is to get to the top, it's even harder to stay there. Flash-in-the-pan status is achieved by many, but sustaining stardom is a whole other ball of wax. Overexposure, burnout, panic, self-destruction, and mismanagement are just a few of the perils that can cause a supernova to fall into eclipse. This also holds true for the business executive on the rise, the wunderkind athlete who is hailed as the future of the sport, the latest fourteen-year-old supermodel, and the hot new waiter who is raking in all the tips.

The attention span of the general public is as fickle and short-lived as a horny fruit fly. For this reason, in any field at all, it is important not to give it all away too soon. One must have a few tricks and surprises up one's sleeve in order to maintain the public's interest. A long-term plan and a sense of evolution are crucial if one is to continue to surprise and fascinate. The scandalous past, the nude photo spread, the revelations of the sad childhood, and the public romances arranged by PR agents must be meted out slowly if there is to be any hope whatsoever of remaining in the spotlight.

Oh, and there's also the work that you do. That counts, too. While it's tempting to stick to a proven formula, all stars must continue to evolve professionally. This is not to say that one should completely abandon that which has proven successful, but one must also be on the lookout for new opportunities for expansion. Of course, not all experiments are successful, but very few ever rise all the way to the top by playing it safe. Corporate CEOs and magazine editors often make the leap to other companies after just a few years before the sparkle of their initial success begins to fade. Athletes switch coaches, actors switch agencies, and horny young newlyweds often trade in spouses. Sometimes these are good decisions, and sometimes they can be disastrous.

Making a change just for the sake of change is never wise. And abandoning your professional or personal allies at the first sign of growth stagnation may be the result of misplaced blame. The athlete who continuously changes coaches because she's not progressing as quickly as she would like may, at some point, need to look in the mirror to get a clear view of the problem. Is she too focused on winning the prize rather than doing the work? Are her expectations unrealistic? Will her impatience ultimately bring about her downfall?

Belief in oneself can easily drift into a sense of entitlement as the intoxication of success begins to kick in. It is heady stuff to be sure. The lust for fame and glory, let alone the achievement of it, can warp our perceptions of where we are in the grand picture. Remember that fame, wealth, and stardom are results; they are not realistic goals. And while it is not misguided to focus on the results, it is a mistake to lose sight of where you are in your personal progression.

Instant success is not only unlikely, it can be very dangerous. It can lead to crippling self-doubt, fear of being revealed as a fraud, or even feelings of guilt, all of which can seriously undermine confidence. A quick start out of the gate is not always the best thing.

Given just a little bit of investigation, most overnight successes are revealed to be just the opposite. It usually turns out that the singer who wins the TV talent competition and lands a recording contract has actually been singing and performing for years, and the gifted athlete who bursts onto the scene has often been groomed since childhood. This is not to suggest that you need lifelong training to succeed, but one thing is certain. You cannot wait to try acting until you get discovered.

So, if you have a clear understanding of your talent, your potential, and, perhaps most important, your limitations, you should be able to make wise decisions once the spotlight beckons. A successful caterer from Connecticut will need to write a few books before launching her own magazine and a media empire. A comedian who dreams of being a serious actor needs to get a few movies under his belt before he tries *Hamlet*. Like a frog jumping lily pads, an overly ambitious leap to a pad too distant can result in a humiliating sink.

SO, WHAT ARE THE GUIDELINES FOR EXPANDING WITHOUT SINKING?

ALWAYS THINK IN TERMS OF BUILDING BLOCKS.

REMAIN OPEN TO PROFESSIONAL ADVICE, BUT TRUST YOURSELF.

RESIST ADVICE TO TRY THINGS THAT YOU KNOW ARE
BEYOND YOU.

NEVER LET FEAR PREVENT YOU FROM TRYING SOMETHING
YOU REALLY WANT TO DO.

LOOK FOR WAYS TO SURPRISE PEOPLE.

REMEMBER THAT REINVENTION CAN REVIVE INTEREST.

RESIST THE URGE TO BECOME COMPLACENT. NOTHING IS
PERMANENT.

TRY TO AVOID THE TEMPTATION TO DO THINGS FOR MONEY
THAT DO NOT INTEREST YOU.

AVOID THE POTENTIAL DELUSION THAT YOU PERSONALLY
ARE MORE IMPORTANT THAN THE WORK.

NEVER HAND OVER YOUR FINANCES TO SOMEONE
ELSE COMPLETELY.

COUNTERACTING BAD PHOTOGRAPHY

ALWAYS WEAR A HAT AND SHADES WHEN YOU LOOK LIKE HELL.

NEVER STAND DIRECTLY UNDER AN OVERHEAD LIGHT.

ALWAYS GIVE THEM AN ANGLE TO PREVENT THAT MUG-SHOT
LOOK.

TRY TO AVOID BEING PHOTOGRAPHED WHEN LAUGHING HYSTERI-
CALLY OR SNEEZING.

LEARN TO HOLD YOUR STOMACH IN TWENTY-FOUR HOURS A DAY.

ALWAYS EXTEND YOUR NECK.

TWIST SLIGHTLY AT THE WAIST TO LOOK SLIMMER.

IN GROUP SHOTS, STAND NEXT TO THE LEAST ATTRACTIVE PERSON.

I don't know much about being a millionaire, but I'll bet I'd be darling at it.
—Dorothy Parker

Money

Given the length of this book, there is insufficient space to list the countless celebrities, athletes, and other luminaries who have rocketed to the top of their respective fields only to end up declaring bankruptcy and appearing on *Hollywood Squares*. In most cases, this is the direct result of a tragic assumption that once a certain level of success is attained, the cash flow will never diminish.

A sudden flood of cash can be very heady stuff, but for those fragile souls who misguidedly believe that newfound wealth makes them a different person, the results are often painfully predictable. Insecurity coupled with naïveté can lead to outlandish spending and excessive generosity that is usually rooted in a childlike desire to validate oneself in the eyes of others. Look at me! Look at me! The ego inflates as the cash flows, the result being a false sense of security and a bloated sense of personal importance. But as Notorious BIG so wisely noted, "Mo' Money, Mo' Problems."

Serious Money

Now that you're a star, you are already on a career track. But remember, you can always hop to another lily pad if yours begins to sink.

After all, Rikki Lake made a lot more money after she abandoned acting to become a talk-show host. You never know. But regardless of whether you are itching to change course or you just want to see what's possible in your current milieu, here is a list of some of the best paid in 2004, by category, according to *Forbes* magazine:

TV HOST: Oprah Winfrey—$210 million

DIRECTOR/PRODUCER: Mel Gibson—$210 million

AUTHOR: J. K. Rowling—$147 million

MALE ATHLETE: Tiger Woods—$80 million

MAGICIAN: David Copperfield—$57 million

MUSICIANS: The Rolling Stones—$51 million

ACTOR: Tom Cruise—$45 million

KID STARS: The Olsen Twins—$28 million

ACTRESS: Angelina Jolie—$27 million

CHEF: Wolfgang Puck—$11 million

FEMALE ATHLETE: Serena Williams—$10 million

TOP MODEL: Heidi Klum—$8 million

SPEAKER: Bill Clinton—$6 million

ONE-YEAR WONDER: Jessica Simpson—$4 million

Depressed? Don't be. Remember that these are the extremes, and we have already discussed the pointlessness of self-comparison. True, the numbers are often obscenely large, but as incomes increase, so do expenses. You need to pay your agent, your lawyer, your trainer, your masseur, the bodyguards, and that fantastic new spiritual guru of yours who got you hooked on those ginseng enemas. And as those expenses rise, so does the level of anxiety about sustaining that income. And when the dry patches come, and they usually do, you had better be prepared.

The most important thing to remember about money is that it is only that—money. And money does not guarantee security, happiness, love, peace, or tranquillity. Sure, it's better to have it than not, but if you can avoid measuring your own success by the state of your bank account, you will have a much happier life. Greed rarely works out well as a primary motivation.

Okay, okay, I know you're getting annoyed because you really do want the money. Fine. That's not unusual. But really, the best way to keep your sanity about money is to keep it in perspective. Remind yourself:

I HAVE BEEN BROKE, BUT I'VE NEVER BEEN POOR.

I AM NOT MY BANK ACCOUNT.

THE MONEY WILL COME WHEN IT COMES.

EVEN WITH TWO DOLLARS IN THE BANK, I CAN STILL CREATE.

MONEY IS FUN, BUT POVERTY IS GREAT FOR THE BIOGRAPHY.

I DON'T NEED TO CHASE AFTER IT; IT WILL FIND ME.

IF THINGS DON'T WORK OUT, I CAN ALWAYS LAND A RICH, OLD SUGAR DADDY/MAMA.

Accepting the Inevitable Shower of Awards

If you have truly put your star power to work over a number of years, be it on-screen, in the workplace, or at PTA meetings, it only follows that gorgeous trophies and awards will surely be bestowed upon you at some point. The manner in which you accept these accolades is of paramount importance. If you are dignified and gracious, you will be adding to the general tone of the presentation, and those who have singled you out for your achievements will be duly pleased. If, on the other hand, you create an excruciatingly embarrassing scene, you may forever ruin your chances of gracing the stage again: "Good lord, we don't want to sit through something like that a second time!"

> **TRY TO REMAIN CALM:** The sight of someone hyperventilating onstage makes the audience very nervous.

> **KEEP YOUR COMPOSURE:** A mild sedative is usually enough to keep the emotional floodgates from bursting open. Sob and the photos will be hideous.

> **SPEAK SLOWLY:** You'll make your points more clearly, and it will hide the fact that you are experiencing a nervous breakdown.

> **FEIGN GRATITUDE:** Whether it's sincere or not is irrelevant. These people took the time to recognize you, so let them see your appreciation and keep the warmth flowing.

DO NOT THANK GOD: First of all, God is not sitting on the edge of a chair thinking, "Will he say my name? Oh, please let him mention me!" And second, if you're that damn spiritual, should you really be falling apart over something so superficial?

PREPARE: No matter how slim your chances of winning, it's always best to have some idea of what you want to say and the people you really need to thank. Besides, no one believes it when award winners say they had nothing prepared.

KEEP YOUR CHIN UP: You'll be very sorry indeed if you look as if you have a fat neck in your moment of glory.

BE HUMBLE: A touch of humility is most charming on such occasions, but if you drift into groveling, the cringe factor will escalate dramatically.

KEEP IT SHORT: A surprisingly short speech is always preferable to a horrifyingly long-winded monologue.

Fame will go by and, so long, I've had you, fame. If it goes by, I've always known it was fickle. So at least it's something I experienced, but that's not where I live.
—Marilyn Monroe

The Nine Stages of Fame

You are on a track, babe. It's usually a very long road, and you can't be fooled into thinking you've arrived at the very first burst of success. Sure, you're excited, and yes, it's really amazing, but you have to understand that fame, like life, is precarious and fickle.

At every stage of the game, it is important to keep an eye on where you stand in the big picture. Stardom, in any of its manifestations, inevitably comes with peaks and valleys, highs and lows, uppers and downers. At any stage of the game, it is very easy to be swept away and fooled into believing that your current state is one of permanence. It isn't.

JUST AS A CAT IS SAID TO HAVE NINE LIVES, SO COMES FAME IN NINE DISTINCT PHASES. ALWAYS REMEMBER WHERE YOU ARE, PUSSYKITTEN.

1. EXHILARATION

TELLTALE SIGNS: Expensive new car, witty quips about the craziness of it all, name-dropping, eye bags, and the continuous picking up of checks in restaurants.

SAMPLE DIALOGUE: "It's so funny! I can't even believe it myself! I'm so glad I have you guys to keep me grounded."

2. FALSE MODESTY

TELLTALE SIGNS: Coy smiles, a terribly earnest interest in others, a love of slumming, and a humble reluctance to draw attention away from the little people.

SAMPLE DIALOGUE: "I'm just very, very lucky, and I'm truly humbled by all that has been given to me. Now tell me about you."

3. EGO EXPANSION

TELLTALE SIGNS: Increased vocal volume, a robust new laugh, a home too large to be fully furnished, and an exhaustingly packed social calendar.

SAMPLE DIALOGUE: "These things don't happen by accident, you know. I earned every bit of my suc-cessssssss."

4. TANTRUMS AND MISBEHAVIOR

TELLTALE SIGNS: Tinted windows, frightened employees, restraining orders filed by ex-lovers, and embarrassing displays of public intoxication.

SAMPLE DIALOGUE: "Why am I surrounded by idiots?! How hard is it to make sure all the grapes are fully peeled?!?"

5. DISENCHANTMENT

TELLTALE SIGNS: Disheveled hair, stretchy clothes, deep friendships forged with bartenders, and shady acquaintances.

SAMPLE DIALOGUE: "This blows. I should have stayed in school."

6. PANIC AND PARANOIA

TELLTALE SIGNS: Flashbulb eyes, multiple bodyguards, canceled appearances, and a large stack of tabloids on the coffee table.

SAMPLE DIALOGUE: "I'm not touching those pears. Do you know how easy it is to inject cyanide into a pear?"

7. SEARCH FOR THE GUILTY

TELLTALE SIGNS: Numerous lawsuits, questionable investments, twelve-step programs, and a confessional television

interview to selflessly warn young people about the danger of drugs.

SAMPLE DIALOGUE: "Don't get me wrong. I do take responsibility for my life, but I was surrounded by leeches and bloodsuckers. I was used. Used, I tell you!"

8. INEVITABLE DECLINE

TELLTALE SIGNS: Wigs, downsizing, dining out with the maid, and the posting of your eight-by-ten headshot at the dry cleaner's.

SAMPLE DIALOGUE: "Where is that scrapbook? Have I shown you my scrapbook?"

9. UNINTENTIONAL SELF-PARODY

TELLTALE SIGNS: An abundance of feathers and sequins, a stockpile of framed photos with famous friends, a tendency to repeat stories, and a sneeze-inducing abuse of cologne.

SAMPLE DIALOGUE: "What, this? It's just an old smoking jacket. Please, come in. The Bordeaux is breathing."

Fer Fook's Sek!

It's exhausting, isn't it? So much to think about, so much to consider. It's like a job, for God's sake. No wonder Cher came down with Epstein-Barr syndrome. I'm exhausted just watching you. Still, one must continue on the path that one has committed to, right? You dreamed it, you saw it, you realized it, and now you have to live with it. But really, doesn't a two-day nap sound positively blissful?

CHAPTER 10

SURVIVING CELEBRITY

Excuse my dust.
—DOROTHY PARKER

Be Careful What You Wish For

You know the old joke. How do you make God laugh? Tell him your plans.

There comes a point in every lifetime when you realize it wasn't what you thought it would be. Your dreams may have been realized, or they may have eluded you. Sometimes, when we let go of a dream, a new life begins and it turns out better than we ever imagined. Then again, sometimes it all just goes in the crapper. But chances are, in hindsight, the story turned out to be pretty interesting. And if you're reading these words, then your heart is still beating, and that means the story is not over. So, ask yourself where you are now:

DO I KNOW WHO I AM?

AM I COMFORTABLE WITH MY PHYSICAL SELF?

AM I CONFIDENT?

DO I APPRECIATE MY INDIVIDUALITY?

DO I UNDERSTAND MY OWN CHARM AND CHARISMA?

AM I IN CONTROL OF THE MESSAGES I'M SENDING?

DO I ENJOY A BIT OF MYSTERY?

CAN I FORGIVE MYSELF MY TAWDRY PAST?

DO I APPRECIATE ALL THAT I HAVE ACHIEVED?

WILL I SURVIVE THIS CRAZY FARCE?

Come on. You know the answer is yes to every one of these questions. And so it should be. But regardless of whether you're just starting out or winding things down, you need to understand that big success always comes with a very high price tag. This should come as no surprise. Of course, there will always be those who prefer to lead quiet, safe, little lives in an effort to minimize the drama and limit the number of surprises. And that's all well and good until they get hit by a bus. I once knew someone who got hit by a bus. It struck me as sad. But then I've always been a very sensitive person.

Anyway, the bottom line is that there's really very little in this life that you can't survive. It's all about the big picture. A superstar like you needs to be strong. Sure, it's exhausting, but what's the alternative? A life without risk is no life at all. Though I must say, I still think bungee jumping is pretty stupid. I mean, yeah, your brain knows you're attached to an elastic cord, but your nervous system doesn't. Seems kind of masochistic. I don't know. I digress.

So, what do you think? Big life or small life? I mean, really, you can live a very big life in complete anonymity, or a small life in the spotlight, right? And let's not forget that things are always changing. Society is evolving in a Darwinian sort of way, and maybe in the future it will be the anonymous who survive, while the famous become an increasingly endangered species. There was a time when air travel was a luxury available to very few. Now, any slob with flip-flops and a backpack can board a plane.

Well, fame hasn't turned into an airbus just yet, so the dreams, the fantasies, and the obsessions live on. There's still some flash to be enjoyed, if you can avoid getting burned by the flame.

The Looking Glass

Did you ever wonder whether, if you could have looked into the future twenty years ago, you would have been amazed, startled, and bewildered to see the picture of your life as it is today? Did your youthful delusions paint a very different picture from the one that actually developed? Would you have been disappointed or wildly impressed? And what might you see if you could look ahead another twenty years? Well, who knows? You flash your own bulb, you make good decisions, and you hope for the best, right?

But you have to wonder, what are you supposed to do if your dreams come true? Where do you go from there? It's one thing to survive the climb, because those distant dreams keep you going, but what happens when you reach the top? Is there even a top? I don't think so. It certainly looks that way when you're standing on the ground looking up, but I'm guessing that's an optical illusion of sorts. Despite appearances, no one ever really defies gravity, and no life is ever finished until it is truly finished.

So, maybe surviving celebrity is really no different than surviving poverty, kidnapping, or divorce. They're all scary. You just have to forge ahead, have a glass of wine, and hope for a good night's sleep. And you ask yourself:

WHAT IS MOST IMPORTANT TO ME?

AM I IN CONTROL OF MY LIFE?

DO I REALLY NEED THE VALIDATION OF OTHERS?

SHOULDN'T I BE MY BEST IN ANY SITUATION?

WOULD I CHOOSE MYSELF AS A FRIEND?

ARE THESE SHOES REALLY WORTHY OF ME?

These are the questions that matter most, my friend. Hold on to your dreams, but let go of your dreamsicles. Enjoy your true story. Remember who you are and charm the shit out of everyone you meet. And if things don't go exactly as you planned, don't worry. They rarely do for anyone. You have to trust that the stars above are guiding the star below.

I've spent an awful lot of time in what I call the empty hotel room.

—Dame Margot Fonteyn

Besides, you're already a star, right? The most important thing is to let the light flow. Unleash your inner celebrity. Make the most of your fifteen minutes. Get Phamous. Milk it. Conquer the spotlight! (Incidentally, just between you and me, these were all considered as actual titles for this book. Can you imagine? I cannot stress enough the importance of the everyday decision. Sheesh!)

Shutting the Door

In the grand theater of Hollywood, it is not uncommon for great stars to reach a point where they decide to pull the curtain down on their own legend. Greta Garbo famously did it, and so did Marlene Dietrich. When they reach this self-determined point of seclusion, it is said that stars have "shut the door." As Dominick Dunne wrote in *Vanity Fair,* this is "an old Hollywood term for when movie actresses, especially great beauties, do a Norma Desmond and cease to appear in public." But the practice is not limited to glamorous actresses. Johnny Carson did it with dignity, and Howard Hughes did it in a spectacularly spooky fashion.

The common thread among those who shut the door would appear to be a need to reclaim their privacy. Visitors are limited to a select few, and the glare of the spotlight is permanently rejected. In some cases it may be prompted by vanity, but more often it is a very simple desire to return to a quiet and peaceful existence where the person reemerges and the star is retired.

Fortunes may dwindle, successes may fall apart, and love sometimes fades away, but it seems that true fame is irreversible. Remember that as you race toward the golden cage.

Disappearing

Now please tell me that you remember our little discussion about leaving the party before the lights come up? You haven't forgotten that, have you? Good. Because there will come a point when it's time to exit the stage, and you can do it gracefully or you can wait for the old vaudeville hook to come and drag you off. Don't let that happen. Regardless of the size of your stardom, or the arena in which you made your mark, a graceful adieu to the spotlight is relatively easy to manage if you simply adhere to the time-tested rules of disappearing:

> **DO** let go of all nonessential staff/entourage.

> **DON'T** let them go without signing nondisclosure agreements.

> **DO** keep the cook and the butler.

> **DON'T** go overboard and end up totally isolated.

> **DO** weed out the idiots.

> **DON'T** lose touch with your pharmacist.

DO keep in touch with your favorite friends.

DON'T suffer any fools.

DO invest in huge sunglasses and a nice selection of hats.

DON'T let photographers catch you off guard.

DO maintain a strict policy regarding visitors.

DON'T allow strangers in who may be concealing cell-phone cameras.

DO retain a personal driver.

DON'T end up in the tabloids because you drove into a tree.

DO find a biographer who will drink with you.

DON'T get stuck reliving your whole life sober.

We Think the World of You

So, look at you now. You really did it. All the things you always believed you needed have been realized. Everyone is watching you. You can't make the slightest mistake without the tabloids jumping on the story. Step out of your bubble of safety and they comment on your weight, your clothes, your demeanor, and the tragic state of your decline. Fantastic.

You're not working anymore, are you? Is your fortune diminishing? Are you over? Has your star diminished? Did you really attend the opening of a supermarket? Why are they all swooping around like vultures over the carcass of a has-been superstar? It's because you

In the end, everything is a gag.
—Charlie Chaplin

signed the unwritten contract of the spotlight, and the higher you flew, the greater the permanent curiosity.

It really is a drag, isn't it? After all, you did give a lot. You worked hard. It's not as if the accolades were just handed to you. Sure, people think it's all glamour, parties, and pretense, but that shit is work. You had to pay the publicist, the stylist, the assistant, the agent, the manager, and every other parasite who profited off your endless hours of dredging up your emotions, tapping your creativity, and spending time with that Nazi of a personal trainer who was, in hindsight, really quite an asshole. And to top it off, they all think you are insanely wealthy. Well, divorce, rehab, and the maintenance of an obscenely large, fully staffed home do not come cheap, do they?

I hear ya, babe. It's messed up. All those years that the public thought you were floating along in some hot-air balloon sipping champagne and devouring caviar were actually a world-class tangle of lawsuits, negotiations, and people dipping into your pot. Wow. It can't have been easy, I mean not at your level of success. I have to say, I am very impressed by your resilience. If it were me, I'd be as bitter as a lemon soaked in diesel fuel.

So, what now? Do you want to work anymore? Do you need to? Maybe you don't need any of this anymore. I mean, really, what's left to prove? Maybe it is time to "shut the door." Why stagger out on the stage for another appearance only to disappoint your fans? Well, I didn't mean to say stagger. You're still amazing, and your walk is still sexy, but you know what I mean. Everyone is obsessed with who you once were. It's like kids who don't realize that they're actually angry with their parents for growing old on them. You're supposed to freeze at forty-two or something.

Maybe the thing to do is to withdraw from the spotlight and write an autobiography. That could help pay for the new kitchen. Did you fuck anyone fabulous? Do you have any dirt on your costars? No, no, no. I'm not suggesting you betray anybody; I'm just saying that people still want to know about you, and if you don't write it all down, someone else will do it for you. I just thought you'd like to have a say in it.

If you don't mind my saying so, I do still worry about you. I think you should try to get out more. I know, you don't want to be photographed anymore, but we talked about a cute wig and some sunglasses, no? Okay, I don't want to push. I totally understand. You've built a legend and you don't want to undermine it by letting people see you age, not that you don't still look fantastic, mind you. But really? You'll never come back?

Oh, I know it's an overused term. And yeah, you're right. Why screw with a masterpiece? Let them remember you at your best, I totally agree. But what about a retrospective of your career? Maybe a lifetime achievement award? Just one last acknowledgment? No? Well, yeah, I see what you mean. It is kind of maudlin. But you realize that the public doesn't understand why you're hiding, right? Okay, okay, don't get upset. I didn't mean hiding, it's just that they're still curious.

About what? Well, you! You had this amazing life and career, and ... yeah, well, right, okay ... normal to you, but ... yes, I understand that everyone's life is extraordinary ... okay. No, I understand. I hear you. I'm sorry.

So, I guess the idea is just to pull a Garbo now? Shut the door for good? Yeah. Well, I think it's pretty admirable. I mean you know what it is to be universally adored, and to let that go, in my opinion, shows a lot of character. Don't laugh. There are lots of public figures who can't even conceive of letting go. I think it's admirable. Fine. Roll your eyes. I still think you're pretty amazing.

Hey, what would you think about just having a few people over for dinner? Just a few friends. You can decide who comes. No pressure. But listen, I do have one favor to ask. I have a friend visiting from out of town, and he's a huge fan. He thinks the world of you, and he would be absolutely thrilled to meet you. Oh, come on. It'll be fun. He's harmless, and I'm sure he'd be more than happy to sit through that god-awful scrapbook of yours.

> *Do not try to live forever. You will not succeed.*
> **—George Bernard Shaw**